FINANCIAL SELF DEFENCE FOR NEW CANADIANS

JOANNE SHAW

ISBN: 978-1-927799-30-7

DISCLOSURE

The following information is given as a general guideline to financial knowledge. It is not intended to give specific financial advice. Please consult a qualified financial planner for specifics of your own personal financial situation. You may find a Certified Financial Planner (CFP) on the Financial Planning Standards Council (FPSC) website at:

http://www.fpsc.ca/find-a-planner-certificant

CONTENTS

Chapters

Appendices

FOREWORD

According to Statistics Canada, Canada is home to approximately 6.8 million immigrants and a diverse population comprising over 200 ethno-cultural groups. One out of five people is a foreign-born immigrant. But like all success stories, there are winners and there are "the rest." This book will contribute significantly to your personal financial success whether you're an immigrant or not. Follow it, and see its impact the next time you have to make a financial decision.

While immigration has played a key role in Canada's successful population growth and economic prosperity, that's not always true for the individual immigrant or their family. Some adapt quickly to our legal, financial and taxation system, especially those from a "western" nation like the UK, France, or Germany. But if they're from Asia, the Middle-East, or Central/South America, the adaptation and assimilation processes can be challenging. For example, struggling to communicate in English or French affects every area of life in which we interact with others. From schooling to jobs, just finding your way around or buying food, language tops the list as a key barrier.

In addition to language and cultural barriers, affordable housing is one of the biggest issues facing Canadians, and can be devastating for a newcomer. Lack of affordable housing in our big cities can make it hard to save and manage money effectively. Research indicates 34-46% of newcomers experience financial vulnerability. The same research also found that, within their first 10 years in Canada, 65% of newcomers experience periods of low income. In some circumstances, a few find it so difficult, still struggling to adjust, that they give up and return to their country.

For this reason I commend Joanne Shaw for writing this book, which is so useful for immigrants who want to make Canada their home. Joanne is a Certified Financial Planner, life coach and yoga instructor. As an all-around life coach, she's helped transform her students, clients, and mentees in innumerable ways - physically, mentally and emotionally. She has personal in-depth knowledge, skills and experience in financial and lifestyle matters affecting new immigrants. This book, the product of her direct observations over the last 20 years working with newcomers, is full of her collected wisdom. The profound influence she's had on individuals and their families inspired her to release this special edition, and I couldn't be happier to endorse her.

Having immigrated myself from Guyana, South America, more than 35 years ago when I was a young adult, I probably broke all the rules essential for sound money management. You name it, I messed it up! Opening my first bank account with high fees, renting an apartment without a lease, buying inappropriate insurance, mistaking a savings account for an investment account, being ignorant of how personal taxation works … I didn't even know that I had to pay tax on my income. A fistfight would have broken out between my supervisor and me if I'd seen the deductions on my first paycheque! I could go on and on, but you get the idea. Guessing, hoping, and ignoring are not effective strategies; knowing and having financial literacy from a trusted source is.

Joanne's work is even more results-oriented regarding financial matters. She's successfully helped her clients to become debt-free, to manage their investments wisely, to be prepared to deal with financial emergencies, to access affordable education savings plans, to support families overseas without financial stress, and ultimately to help immigrants realize the dream of owning their own home.

As a Certified Financial Planner myself, and in my work in Canada and around the world, I've seen firsthand that those who know the rules on financial matters (whether via this book or a financial professional) achieve better outcomes over both the short and long term. My own experience has led me to believe that, on average, Canadians lack the education and knowledge necessary to confidently make financial decisions. Had someone handed me a book like this, upon arrival or soon after, I would have avoided some costly and irreversible financial mistakes.

Looking back, my decisions were laughable and costly, but I survived - and you will too! It's surprising how a little knowledge and commitment can help you adapt to your new environment. If coming to Canada were a game, this book will provide you directions on how to navigate the financial maze and finish successfully. I firmly believe people don't plan to fail in life, *they fail to plan*. But by investing a little time via this book to develop your financial literacy, you'll have the essential elements to make sound financial decisions. And when it makes sense, you can also consult a trusted advisor so that big ticket items can be bought wisely.

Despite the initial obstacles, immigration to Canada will continue to blossom, thanks to our almost-free health care, a great educational system, a clean and beautiful environment, and our overall quality of life. Learning some financial planning strategies through Joanne's down-to-earth communication style will enhance that experience even more.

My hope for you, dear reader, is for you to succeed in adapting to the challenges facing you, and to build a stable life in Canada, especially in terms of your financial well-being!

D. Tony Mahabir, MBA, CMC, CFP, CIM, RRC

CEO, Canfin Financial Group of Companies

Toronto, Ontario, Canada

ACKNOWLEDGMENTS

I've had the great fortune to be born a Canadian and thus enjoy all of the privileges that implies. I've also had the pleasure of being surrounded by people of different cultures and backgrounds from all over the world. The diversity of my country is one of the many things that make me proud to say: "I am Canadian." Several dear friends inspired this book: Dolores, Jeffrey, Roberto, Roseli, Manpreet, and Maithili, to name just a few.

Writing a book takes time, effort and assistance. I must thank my editor Alan Annand and graphic artist Linda Tenenbaum, without either of whom I'd be lost. I also thank my family for their support and patience. Most of all, I want to thank my friend and business associate Tony Mahabir for writing the foreword and for sharing his knowledge on being a new Canadian.

I hope this book gives you guidance and peace of mind as you navigate your new world. Welcome to Canada!

- Joanne Shaw, BA, CFP

INTRODUCTION

It takes a very special type of person to be able to pack up your life and leave your home country. I have the utmost respect for anyone who has the fortitude, sense of adventure and courage to move their entire life to a new country. Some are seeking a better life for themselves; some are interested in giving their children future opportunities they might never have had in their current home country. Regardless of the reason that people immigrate, I'm in awe of the challenges and struggles they face. I've written this book with the hope that your transition to Canada will be made just a little bit easier by providing some basic financial information relevant to all Canadians, new and old. I wish you the best of luck and I hope that you're able to fulfill all of your dreams.

As a martial artist I know a few things about self-defence. As a CFP (Certified Financial Planner) I know a few things about financial literacy and financial planning. Since there's a lack of knowledge about both these areas, I decided to meld the two loves of my life into one succinct book. I hope to encourage and educate new Canadians to the best of my abilities because, just as in self-defence, *only you can protect yourself*!

In martial arts, becoming more physically self-assured and empowered is very important. In life it's equally important to become financially self-sufficient and empowered. As we progress I'll use the basics of self-defence as a platform to provide guidelines for your financial self-defence.

As a financial planner, it's always amazed me that clients who believe they'll make money actually do so, while those who think otherwise are equally correct. Two different clients may enter the market at the same time with the same investments and yet the outcome will differ. This defies logic. One explanation I can offer is that the client's belief system and the emotional energy they're attracting into their lives are having a major influence on the outcome of their investing. Ultimately the client's expectations for payoff, and/or their discipline to persevere (or not) with an investment program during market fluctuations is the greatest determinant of their return.

Much of what we believe and many of our emotions regarding money are the result of money attitudes we witnessed as we were growing up. In general we either fully adopt our parents' attitudes about money or we reject them completely and rebel. Either way, we seldom sit down and make a rational decision about what our attitude and belief system is when it comes to money and finance.

Everyone has heard the expression, "Money is the root of all evil." The truth is it's really the worship of money that is the root of all evil. There are many examples of corrupt corporations that are only out for a buck at the expense of anyone or anything such as the environment, human rights, etc. Where there is no social consciousness attached to money it's easy to abuse the power that money wields.

Having money can be the wellspring of many good deeds. If you have enough money you can live the lifestyle you desire, have more free time to do the things you love, and have extra money to spend on those you love. Having plenty of money can afford you the luxury of contributing to charities or causes important to you as well.

The truth is there's enough money and food to go around for everyone. The degree to which you'll attract money into your life may perhaps be influenced by how much you feel you deserve money and abundance.

If you grew up in a home where money was scarce and it was a constant battle to survive, then subconsciously you may feel that you don't deserve abundance in your life. This is a self-fulfilling prophecy. You know the expression: "Whatever I can conceive and believe I can receive." Well, that works for good things and bad, so be careful what you focus on.

It's been my observation that we attract into our lives the things we believe subconsciously. Sometimes our beliefs will overrule our conscious thoughts. The best way to reprogram your subconscious is to purposely think positive about exactly what you want to attract into your life. At the very worst, you could have some pleasant thoughts.

If you grew up in a home with an abundance of money then you may have a sense of entitlement. You may expect abundance in your life and feel you deserve it. Some children raised in homes with unlimited money have no idea how to make a living or be self-sufficient because from a financial standpoint every need in their lives has been met. Money requires a level of responsibility no matter how much or little there is. Some children from wealthy families reject the whole money thing or become reckless and irresponsible about money.

In terms of money, no matter what type of home you grew up in, you may have a similar or totally different attitude than your family. But have you ever analysed your own personal relationship with money? This is what I call your own personal *money consciousness.*

CHAPTER 1:
MONEY CONSCIOUSNESS

Most people spend more time deciding where to go for their next vacation than planning their financial success. Have you ever sat down and assessed your relationship with money and finances? Do you know what's really important to you from a financial standpoint? Have you any idea how much money you'll need to retire. Have you even thought about it?

First let's try to address what I mean by money consciousness. Here's my definition:

Money Consciousness is being fully aware of your core belief system in terms of your personal relationship with money.

So how do we determine our personal money consciousness? Let's begin by thinking back. When I'm asked to speak to groups about money consciousness I do a guided meditation to help everyone identify the core beliefs and messages about money when they were growing up. I have them take a few deep breaths, close their eyes and think back to when as a child or young teen they overheard a conversation about money. This may have been between their parents or siblings or anyone of significance in their lives.

What's most important is to get a sense of the emotions and atmosphere in which the conversation took place. Was this a relaxed conversation? Was there a lot of tension? Was it a calm discussion or an argument? Was there a feeling of lack or abundance? Was there a sense of accountability and a feeling that things would be all right? How did this conversation influence you? Can you see the connection between that "message" about money and your current financial situation or your current financial beliefs?

People rarely sit down and think about their own personal relationship with money. Money is a form of energy and a source of power. It's also an essential part of life. You probably have a good idea about what your ideal house would look like or your favourite dream car. But do you know how you subconsciously process information about money? When you spend too much money do you have buyer's remorse or do you have a sense that everything will be fine because you have abundance in your life? What message about money did you receive from family and close friends? When someone mentions the words "financial planning" do you run and hide or do you welcome the opportunity to learn more and make educated decisions?

After you've evaluated influences from the past, it's time to think about the present. What does money represent to you? What emotions come up when you talk about money? Are you relaxed or do you feel totally overwhelmed? Would you like to have a better handle on your financial situation? Has the power of money in your life been a negative or a positive?

Some people feel that if they have too much money it'll corrupt them. This may hold true for some people, but not necessarily for you. Why would money corrupt you? If you're a good, caring and compassionate person, that's not going to change because you have more money. On the contrary, having more money gives you freedom to do what you like, provide better care to those you love, and affords you the luxury to give more back to the world.

For example, it costs $10,000 to install a potable water source in a town in Haiti so people don't have to walk 15 km to get fresh water. If you had more money wouldn't it be wonderful to just send $10,000 to help those in need? Everyone deserves to have access to fresh water daily. I don't know what your passion is or if you've even had time to think about it but I'm sure you could think of a cause that you would like to support. You may want to send money back to your home country to support family members. Perhaps you'd like to give more to support animal shelters, help the homeless, feed the hungry or donate to your place of worship.

Money consciousness is about what you consciously perceive as the power of money and what you'd do with it. We rarely change our core belief system because we're rarely objective enough to challenge our core beliefs. The key to identifying your own money consciousness is to determine where your core belief about money came from, and determine if this is really your own money consciousness or someone else's.

The following exercises are designed to help you understand your own money consciousness. People rarely have time for these things but please take a coffee break or a night off and dedicate it to learning about your own money consciousness. If nothing else, you'll have a better idea about your own personal relationship with money and what it means to you. I suspect that it'll also help to make you feel just a little bit more empowered.

Money Consciousness Exercise 1:

Complete this checklist, ticking Yes or No for each statement.

Category 1	**YES**	**NO**
I feel in control of my finances		
I've determined my own money consciousness		
I feel confident I have enough money to retire when the time comes		
My partner and I both understand our current financial situation		
I'm very generous with my money and I give to many charities		
I plan my finances for the future and I currently have a saving program		
I'm confident I understand my financial situation for now and the future		
Category 2		
I'd like to have a better understanding of my current financial situation		
I don't like to think about money, I get very anxious and confused		
I tend to shop when I'm depressed because it makes me feel better		

I feel helpless in trying to get ahead financially		
I lend money to other people when I shouldn't		
I often buy things that I don't really need but I love to shop		
I don't feel that I understand my finances all that well		

If you answered YES to four or more questions in Category 1 you're well on your way to financial security. If you answered YES to four or more questions in Category 2 then it's probably a good thing you're reading this book.

Money Consciousness Exercise 2:

Sit in a quiet place and take a few deep breaths. Write a list of personal statements about money - what it means to you and what it represents in your life.

Here's an example of how you might summarize your Money Consciousness:

- $ My attitude about money was most influenced by my father
- $ I have a positive attitude about having money and abundance in my life
- $ I feel I deserve to have abundance in my life
- $ I've always felt that I'll need to work hard to get ahead

- $ Having lots of money means I'll be able to give more to charities I support
- $ Abundance in my life is from having a strong family life and good friends
- $ Money enables me to provide for my family and for my future retirement

Another great exercise is to get up every morning and write down your life objectives in the present tense. For example: *I currently have four hundred thousand dollars in investible assets in my retirement plan.* This may not be the case but write it down as if it's already happened. These are positive affirmations but you're also programming your mind and heart to fulfill these desires.

Determining your personal money consciousness and what money means to you, is your first level of awareness in financial planning.

CHAPTER 2: AWARENESS

Awareness is the first important aspect of physical self-defence. Know where you are, know where you want to go, and know how you're going to get there. From a self-defence standpoint, let people know where you're going and when you'll arrive. If you're late, someone will be wondering why and will raise concerns that you're missing.

The goal in self-defence is very simple: Always be aware of your surroundings so that you're never in a situation that is threatening or could compromise your safety. Awareness is the number one objective of self-defence. By being aware at all times you'll be in the best possible position to either avoid danger entirely or deal with whatever situation comes up. (*See Appendix 2 for a list of awareness and avoidance strategies for personal self-defence.)*

The same attitude holds true for finances. Awareness in financial terms would include knowing the following:

- ✓ What are your lifetime goals?
- ✓ How can you translate them into financial goals?
- ✓ What is your net worth? (Balance sheet of assets less liabilities)
- ✓ What is your current cash flow? (Income less expenses)
- ✓ When do you expect to retire?
- ✓ What will you do in retirement - find a part time job, travel or play golf?
- ✓ How much money will you need to retire? (the magic number)
- ✓ What rate of return on your investments will you need to meet your goals?
- ✓ How much money do your children need to get a post-secondary education?

Although this may sound intimidating, by the end of this book these questions will seem pretty basic. So let's start raising your financial awareness.

Financial goals

Everyone is unique in terms of why money is important to them. My friend Dan would love to buy a monster power boat with all the gear. As for myself, I don't even like the noise of motor boats, and don't care if I ever own one. I'd prefer to have a canoe because I'm a wilderness camper.

Bottom line: no one else can tell you what your financial goals are or what they should be.

Here are some examples of financial goals clients have told me about over the years:

- ✓ I want to buy a house/car/cottage/rental property, or renovate the house, or (fill in the blank) ____________.
- ✓ We're expecting our first baby and we want to be sure we have enough money.
- ✓ I want to ensure that when I die my wife will have everything she needs.
- ✓ When I retire I want to go back to university and get a Master's degree.
- ✓ I'm fine as long as I have enough money to get my children a good education.
- ✓ Since my mother lived to 102, I want to make sure my money doesn't run out before I do.

Try to focus on what's really important to you. If contributing to your favourite charity every year is critical to your happiness, then that's a financial goal. On the other hand, having five hundred TV channels to choose from may not be as crucial. If you're not sure what your goals are, look to your core values and see if they give you some ideas. Another option is to do the "Headstone" test. If you only had six months left to live, how would you change your lifestyle to meet your priorities? Would you go for something you've always dreamed of doing, or sit down and write a will?

If you're still drawing a blank, then perhaps getting a professional financial planner to prepare a comprehensive financial plan will help bring things into focus. I've had situations in which clients have told me their life goals prior to doing their complete financial plan. After completing and presenting their plan to them, they altered their life goals based on the information I provided. I feel privileged and honoured to have been able to provide such an influence in people's lives.

Exercise: *Sit in a quiet place, take a few deep breaths and make a list of your life goals. It helps to have a short-, mid- and long-term list of goals. Five or 10 years from now, your priorities may be quite different from what they are today. This is a good exercise to repeat every few years to see how priorities change with time and circumstances. Your life goals can be translated into financial goals by a financial plan.*

An example of some life goals that can be translated into financial terms would look like this:

Life Goal	**Financial target**	**Estimated deadline:**
Provide my children with a post-secondary education:	$80,000 each for two children = $160,000	2026
Retire by age 65	$1,500,000 in assets	2036
Purchase a new car	$40,000	2019
Pay off the mortgage	$350,000	2032

This exercise will help to solidify your priorities and summarize your overall financial needs for the future. As mentioned, this is a moving target so your objectives should be reviewed on a regular basis.

Now let's get technical in terms of your financial awareness!

Income and expenses: where do I stand?

It's critical to know where you are now in terms of your financial situation. No matter how much income you make, if you don't know where it's going, you're at risk. It's so important to understand how much money's coming in, how much is going out and, of course, what's left over!

Every person is unique when it comes to financial record-keeping. I had one client who provided a detailed spreadsheet showing everything, right down to each cup of coffee and newspaper, purchased over the years. I had another client who stored years worth of financial records in a large cardboard box that sat on the dining room table. Following each question I asked, we'd search for the appropriate information in that big box.

No matter what, we all need a certain level of organization in our lives, but especially when it comes to finances. You need to know where your money's going, what you're spending it on and how the amounts balance with your income. A cash flow statement accounts for everything coming and going - income and expense.

Income

Practicing financial self defence involves many aspects of your life. Having an income is like having oxygen. But having a career today isn't like generations ago, when our parents and grandparents had jobs for life. My father retired with an indexed pension from the same job he held for 36 years. He never had to worry about having sufficient funds for his retirement. Those days are long gone for most of us.

The majority of layoffs today happen to people in their fifties. This age group earns a high salary, so corporations think, why keep someone that age and salary when you can hire a couple of people in their twenties for less money? Now what does a 50-something do when they're out of work and still 15 years away from collecting a government pension?

Sadly, most companies are reluctant to hire older employees. The Canadian Government Human Resource guidelines caution against age discrimination but in reality companies hire whomever they want and justify it however they can. From an income or job standpoint, how do we defend ourselves?

One of the ways to defend yourself and your income is to diversify and expand your options. Here are some suggestions:

- Learn more than one area of expertise
- Go back to school
- Get certified in something else
- Start your own small business

- Expand your knowledge base to become a valued expert in your field
- Don't be afraid to try something new

You're the only one who can guarantee your employability. If I didn't work in finance I could teach yoga or Reiki (a form of therapeutic touch that aids in relaxation and the healing process), give Reiki treatments, get a sales job, scrub floors or wait on tables. Having many options to earn money is what I call "job-proofing" yourself.

Do what you love and the money will follow. Once we make up our minds about something, there's a type of synchronization with the universe. Ever noticed that when you finally commit to an idea/action/cause, things begin aligning to support you?

Your idea can be good or bad. If you spend your life saying "Well, I could never do that" or "I'm too old to go back to school", then you have a self-fulfilling prophesy. If you focus on "I can be independent and have a successful business" or "I know I'll do well in college even though I hated high school", then you'll have a self-fulfilling prophesy.

To identify your passion, think about a time in your life when you were doing something and the hours flew by. Were you happy and relaxed? Did time stand still? If so, this is one of your passions. Explore it. How could you make money from it? Could you turn a volunteer service into a paying job?

Opening your mind to opportunity is the first challenge but there are social stereotypes and belief systems

regarding age and aging. Avoid hardening of the attitude.

I've made major changes in my life several times. It was never easy but always worth the effort. I completely changed careers at age 47. I walked away from a well-paid corporate job to something in which I had no prospects, no income and no way of knowing if I'd make it. I faced risk and a huge learning curve, but it was the smartest choice I ever made.

Do your homework, go for it and trust in the universe to provide. But ensure you have a fallback position and some money in reserve to support you.

If you're already in your dream job, celebrate that every day. If you like what you do but complain anyway, maybe you need a change of attitude. Stop and smell the roses.

Once we have a job with some income, we can consider how to put it to work. Determining net or disposable income is straightforward for most people.

On every employee's pay stub are shown the gross salary minus any deductions the employer is required to withhold. The typical deductions are:

- $ Income taxes
- $ Contributions to EI (Employment Insurance)
- $ Contributions to CPP (Canadian Pension Plan)
- $ Contributions to a company pension plan
- $ Contributions to a group RRSP (Registered Retirement Savings Plan)
- $ Premiums for company medical plans

In addition to these common deductions at source, employees can also have their employer make regular deductions for a wide range of financial transactions, eg, company stock ownership plan, purchase of Canada Savings Bonds, registered charities, employee purchase discounts, etc.

If you're self-employed or receive commission income, it gets more complicated. The key is to know what you can use for tax deductions (home office, phone bills, mileage, percent of hydro, etc). Many deductions are quite legitimate from a tax perspective. In some cases, if you're a commissioned salesperson, you may need a letter from your company confirming you work from home or use your car for business purposes. There are several ways to reduce your taxable income and I highly recommend getting your taxes done professionally at least once to ensure you take advantage of all the tax breaks available to you.

Other sources of income include:

<u>The Canadian child tax benefit</u>

The Canada child tax benefit (CCTB) is a non-taxable amount paid monthly to help eligible families with the cost of raising children under 18 years of age. To be eligible, you must meet the following conditions:

- you must live with the child, and the child must be under the age of 18;
- you must be primarily responsible for the care and upbringing of the child;

- you must be a resident of Canada and a Canadian citizen, and your spouse or common-law partner must be a Canadian citizen, a permanent resident, a protected person, or a temporary resident who's lived in Canada for the previous 18 months, and who has a valid permit in the 19th month. (*Note: Special rules apply to shared custody.)*

The Goods and services tax/Harmonized sales tax (GST/HST) credits

The GST/HST credit is a tax-free quarterly payment that helps individuals and families with low or modest incomes offset all or part of the GST or HST that they pay.

Ontario trillium benefit (OTB)

(Note: each province has its own available tax credits which vary by province)

The Ontario trillium benefit (OTB) is the combined payment of the Ontario energy and property tax credit, the Northern Ontario energy credit, and the Ontario sales tax credit. The annual OTB entitlement is usually divided by 12 and the payments issued monthly. The OTB program is legislated and funded by the Province of Ontario. The Canada Revenue Agency administers this program on behalf of the province.

CPP (Canadian Pension Plan) income

Almost all individuals who work in Canada contribute to the Canada Pension Plan (CPP). The CPP provides pensions and benefits when contributors retire, become disabled, or die. Please note that the amount of money received from CPP is directly related to the number of years you have worked in Canada.

Retirement pension

You can apply for and receive a full CPP retirement pension at age 65 or 67 depending upon your current age or receive it as early as age 60 with a reduction, or as late as age 70 with an increase.

Post-retirement benefit

If you continue to work while receiving your CPP retirement pension, your CPP contributions will go toward post-retirement benefits, which will increase your retirement income. If you are self-employed you'll need to make both employee and employer contributions to the CPP plan. If you're self-employed and you continue to work after you begin receiving CPP, you'll have to continue making payments into the CPP plan for another two (2) years minimum, while continuing to work.

As a Canadian citizen qualified to receive CPP payments, you may live anywhere in the world and continue to receive your payments without restriction. However, if you wish to take advantage of the universal health care system in Canada you'll need to live in Canada for six months of the year.

If you have teenagers working before age 18, they're not obligated to make CPP payments. If their employer deducts CPP from them, your teen should file their own tax return and declare that they are CPP exempt. The CPP payments will then be refunded. Your child will only benefit from CPP contributions made after age 18, so it's best to file a return. You can ask the employer not to deduct the CPP in the first place, but not all employers are willing to change their system.

CPP Disability Income

The Canada Pension Plan (CPP) provides a taxable monthly payment as a disability benefit to people who've made enough contributions to the CPP and who are disabled and can't work any job on a regular basis. Benefits may also be available to their dependent children. In order to receive the CPP disability tax credit and to apply for CPP disability, you must obtain a letter from your doctor to confirm that you are unable to work.

Children's benefit

The children's benefit is a monthly benefit for dependent children (under age 18, or between 18 and 25 and attending school full time) of someone receiving a CPP disability benefit.

Old Age Security Pension

The Government of Canada has introduced measures to gradually increase the age of eligibility for the OAS pension and the Guaranteed Income Supplement (GIS) between the years 2023 and 2029, from 65 to 67. *People currently receiving OAS benefits will not be affected by the changes.*

Under the change, anyone born in 1963 or later will be eligible for the Old Age Security pension and Guaranteed Income Supplement benefits at the age of 67.

The Old Age Security Pension (OAS) is a monthly pension paid to most Canadians aged 65 or older who've lived in Canada for more than 10 years. The funding for this benefit comes from general tax revenue and is controlled by the federal government.

As of June 2018 the maximum OAS monthly payment is $589.59 per month, and is recalculated each quarter to the consumer price index (CPI).

OAS is clawed back starting at $75,910 of individual (not family) net taxable income. The claw-back is done on a percentage basis, but isn't as severe as people think since it's based on net taxable income. Individuals who have net taxable incomes of $123,019 and above have 100% of their OAS benefit clawed back - receiving none of it. The OAS benefit is aimed at those individuals who are in the low and moderate-income brackets.

Guaranteed Income Supplement (GIS)

The Guaranteed Income Supplement is a tax-free payment available to seniors with very low incomes. Its funding comes from general tax revenue and is controlled by the federal government. Eligibility for the program is from July 1 to June 30, following the filing of the prior year's tax return, and based on that return's taxable income. *You must apply for this benefit.*

If you qualify, the government will send you an application. As of June 2018 the maximum monthly benefit is $880.61 for a single person with an annual income of $17,880 or less.

Your total net income reflects the various deductions from your paycheque. In addition, you may receive separate payments from the government for some of the above special sources of income. Please note that guidelines currently in place may change at any time.

Expenses

Once we know our net income, ie, what money's coming in, we must examine what's going out. In financial terms, our expenses are an account of what we spend money on.

I've had clients who had no idea what they were regularly spending money on. If you're one of those people, I recommend keeping a folder or large envelope somewhere handy. Get a receipt for everything you spend money on and put it in the envelope. Have an envelope for each month.

Then you can, for example, take your separate envelopes for July, August and September, add up all the receipts and take the average. (Eg, July + August + September = total Q3 expenses, and divided by three = average monthly expense for that period.) Many large businesses measure their results by the quarter. This will give you a sense of your average monthly expenses, and is a good starting point to be aware of your cash flow.

Whenever a client buys a new home or has a baby, I ask them to go through at least three months of spending before doing a comprehensive financial plan. In so doing, they'll encounter the majority of expenses they'll typically have on an ongoing basis. This gives us a good foundation upon which to base their plan. A comprehensive financial plan will outline your income and expenses, your balance sheet with net worth, the required amount of money needed during retirement, education savings required, tax and estate strategies, and investment-holding analysis and recommendations.

Having completed a comprehensive financial plan for my clients, I've had different outcomes. Here are just a few examples:

- The client discovered a surplus of over $2,000 a month that wasn't accounted for
- The clients were spending $1,000 more per month than they were earning
- The client had a good cash flow with savings at month's end that could be invested
- The clients realized they could afford to buy a term insurance policy for their family

- The clients determined they could contribute $50 a month into an RESP
- The clients realized they could double what they were saving for their retirement
- The clients realized their retirement was fully funded and they didn't have to worry
- One client was shocked to discover she was worth a million dollars

In case you haven't figured it out by now, each client is unique.

A financial plan is a moving target. You can't just do a plan once in a lifetime. Life happens and things change. Most major life events will affect your financial plan, so ongoing monitoring and updating is important.

When it comes to spending money, there's only one rule to ensure sustainability:

SPEND LESS THAN YOU MAKE

This sounds simple but it's not for people who struggle to make ends meet. Priorities are a key element in your spending pattern. There will be situations in which immediate gratification must be postponed for the sake of good financial positioning. If you know where you are and where you want to go, you're in a much better position to make these key buying decisions.

Shelter, food and other basics of life constitute the majority of ongoing costs. In this day and age most people (especially the young) think mobile phone plans and other gadgets are also an essential part of life. Some of my most sophisticated clients still forget to account for personal care costs, eg, haircuts, facials, manicures, clothing, spa days, etc. Other things like children's piano lessons or sports fees may also be overlooked.

A Cash Flow Statement

A Cash Flow Statement is a declaration of all your regularly recurring expenses. (*See Appendix 3 for your expense worksheet.*) Typically this would include the following key items:

- $ Mortgage or rent payment
- $ Taxes and/or condo fees
- $ Utilities: hydro, gas, water
- $ Loan or line-of-credit payments (*If you're borrowing to invest, you get a tax deduction for interest paid on the loan, but keep this loan separate from other loans or lines of credit so that you can prove its applicability in case of an audit*)
- $ Car loan or lease payments
- $ Gas for car
- $ Parking and public transit
- $ Dependent care costs, for either children or elderly parents
- $ Maintenance costs for home and car
- $ Cable, internet, home phone, mobile
- $ Gifts and charitable donations
- $ Sports and fitness dues/fees
- $ Entertainment
- $ Personal care

- $ Travel
- $ Insurance of many types:
  - ▪ Property and casualty - for car and home protection
  - ▪ Life insurance
  - ▪ Critical illness insurance
  - ▪ Disability insurance
  - ▪ Long-term care insurance

Hopefully, the following savings are also part of your ongoing expenses but are considered by many to be optional:

- RRSP contributions toward retirement savings
- RESP (Registered Education Savings Plan) contributions
- Emergency fund (not really optional, but often neglected)

Once we have our net income and our total expenses, we simply subtract the second from the first. Hopefully there's more income than expenses at month's end. This is the essential financial information you need to build your financial defence.

While the above is a simple approach to determining your cash flow, the reality is rarely this straightforward. Why? Because life happens!

What about tuition fees for your child's education? A new roof on the house, car repairs you hadn't counted on or a $2,000 dental bill can derail the best-laid financial plans.

Living within your means can be challenging because often things don't work out as planned. That's why it was mentioned earlier that having an emergency fund really isn't an option. Scenarios like those above can completely derail the best-intended financial plans. The only way to be prepared is to have some form of emergency fund. The rule of thumb is to have 3-6 months of income available at all times.

This isn't always possible but, if you're disciplined with your money, you could have an *unused* line of credit. In other words, get a credit card or establish a line of credit that you only use for emergencies. This is your "hide it away for a rainy day" line of credit. Ideally, have three months of income set aside in a safe investment like a high-yield savings account or a TFSA (Tax Free Savings Account). This strategy will let you sleep at night.

Having an emergency fund is a useful form of *avoidance.* In other words, avoid getting in a situation where you can't make ends meet nor pay the bills to survive. More about avoidance later...

Net worth: your personal balance sheet

Now that we know our income and expenses it's time to determine our *net worth.* Your net worth is an assessment of your financial fitness. In the context of physical fitness, it's your body mass index reading.

Your net worth is determined from a balance sheet. It includes all your assets and liabilities. Your net worth is the difference between the two.

In other words, if you had to sell off things you owned in order to pay off every debt, how much money would you have left?

Assets

Assets are things of value we own. I stress ownership because when you lease a car you don't own it. Therefore it's not an asset. But if you purchased a car it's considered an asset because if you had to you could sell it for money. Your home and car are generally your largest assets.

Hard assets typically include:

- $ Home
- $ Cottage
- $ Car
- $ Boat, Sea-doo, Ski-doo, etc
- $ Furniture
- $ Sports equipment
- $ Valued collectibles
- $ Jewelry/furs

Remember: hard assets are things you could sell for money but it could take time, or you might be forced to sell when the value is low.

Liquid assets are typically investments that are easily liquidated, giving immediate access to cash, for example:

- $ RRSP

- $ RESP
- $ Savings account
- $ Chequing account
- $ GICs (Guaranteed Investment Certificates)
- $ Cash surrender value of an insurance policy
- $ Stocks, bonds, mutual funds
- $ TFSA, open investments

Liabilities

Liabilities are your debt obligations. These include any expense to pay off money owed, eg, the loan from your sister. The most common liabilities are related to the purchase of major assets:

- $ Your mortgage, and/or second mortgage
- $ Your car loan (not a lease, because it doesn't result in ownership)
- $ Your active line of credit
- $ Anything purchased over time via a store purchase plan
- $ Credit card balance due
- $ Repayments toward investment loans

Net worth

The calculation for net worth is simple:

1. Add up the current market value of all your assets (eg, house $435,000, car $15,000)

2. Add up all your liabilities (eg, mortgage $230,000, balance on car loan $6,000)

3. Calculate the difference:

Assets:	$430,000 + $15,000 =	$445,000
Liabilities:	$230,000 + $6,000 =	$236,000
Net Worth:		$209,000

As of 2018, the average net worth for Canadians is $333,715.

Your net worth is the X-ray of your financial health. It's impossible to know someone's net worth by looking at what they have. In order to "keep up with the Joneses" their big house may be fully mortgaged and their Audi leased. Even though they may look richer, their net worth may be less than yours.

To measure your headway from a financial standpoint, calculate your net worth at least once a year. This will show if your assets are increasing in value as your debt goes down, not the other way around!

Let's summarize our financial awareness. At this point you should have:

- ✓ An outline of your personal "money consciousness"
- ✓ A statement of financial goals for yourself and/or your family
- ✓ A cash flow statement (all income and expenses)
- ✓ A balance sheet that shows your net worth

This is a great base upon which to build your financial strategy, to know you're aware of your current and potential financial status.

In a perfect world, knowing the above would be enough to guarantee financial success. However, like any journey, there are things to be avoided on the road to financial success, so let's take time to discuss *avoidance*.

CHAPTER 3: AVOIDANCE

Avoidance is another key aspect of personal and financial self-defence. The best way to minimize getting into trouble is to be aware, in advance, of compromising situations. Before the real trouble begins, prepare in advance for the pitfalls. See Appendix 2 for ideas regarding personal self-defence.

From a financial standpoint, preventing financial hardship includes:

- Living within your means
- Having an emergency fund
- Being properly insured
- Having estate planning in place
- Saving for the future

The first segment on awareness will help in terms of living within your means and having an emergency fund. Next we need to deal with a few inevitable issues, like death and taxes. We'll look into taxes later but for now, let's consider what would happen in the event of death.

It's important to determine exactly what effect this would have on your financial situation. Some other things that might also affect you financially are severe illness or disability, both of which can be more financially devastating than death.

If you die, there'll be certain one-time expenses, eg, burial, estate taxes, etc, that will be borne by your survivors. For example a funeral may cost $25,000, while estate and probate taxes may add up to another $40,000. This is a one-time expense borne by the estate and settled at that time. However, if you're ill or disabled, it may cost you $10,000 for therapy, and $5,000 for drugs, and $12,000 for assisted-care living, for the 10 years you might yet live, and where is the money for all of that going to come from when you're unable to work?

There are two key means of avoiding financial despair: insurance, and a good estate plan.

Insurance

The general purpose of insurance it is to compensate you for unexpected loss. You can protect yourself and your family with life insurance, critical illness insurance, disability insurance, property and casualty insurance.

Life insurance

In most cases a basic term life insurance policy is sufficient to protect against loss of income or pay taxes on your estate. A term policy has no savings component and you're covering yourself in case of death only for a set period after which time the policy is finished and no longer needed. A general term insurance policy is much preferred over a specific mortgage insurance policy which typically pays down your mortgage at the time of death. A universal life insurance policy is a special type of policy with a savings component and specific tax strategies useful to small business owners. For pure protection and economy, a term insurance policy is generally sufficient for most families.

There are two reasons you need life insurance: to protect your family and preserve your capital.

If you're like most people with young children and a mortgage, you'd like to help your family maintain their current lifestyle even if you die. For example, if you're in your forties with two children, and both you and your partner are working, consider the consequences if one or both of you passed away.

To estimate what's needed to maintain a lifestyle, start by examining your cash flow. What if one of you weren't there, and half your family income disappeared? Although some costs might disappear, (eg, operating and maintaining a second car) other bills would still come in regardless.

Even though you might have only one income, generally you want to stay in your home, pay the bills and contribute to your child's RESP. A properly assessed insurance policy with sufficient coverage will do the job. The recommended period of coverage depends on a few things: How old are you? How much longer will you work? When will you pay off your mortgage? When do your children plan to go to college?

Life insurance is just good commonsense when you have a home, a family, and young children. Even if you have a stay-at-home mom, she should be covered with Life and Critical Illness insurance. If she can't take care of the children, there'll be money to hire someone.

Your age, state of health and whether or not you smoke are key factors in the cost of life insurance premiums, ie, payments to purchase insurance.

Another reason to buy life insurance is to cover taxes on your estate. If your estate is worth a million dollars or more, you should have insurance on your estate to cover the taxes when you die. If you're not insured and you die with a million-dollar estate, the government will probably get about half of it, depending upon where the money is invested. But a $500,000 policy would cover the estate taxes at the time of death and your family would inherit your full estate.

Whatever life insurance you buy, make sure it's underwritten at the time of purchase. Underwriting means they'll do a medical exam prior to issuing the policy. Get the policy underwritten or risk not having a claim paid at a future date. A claim is made to the insurance company for payment of the face value of the insurance policy upon the death of the insured person.

Mortgage insurance

A mortgage insurance policy will pay off your mortgage if you die. This sounds good, so you'd think it's the best way to protect yourself. Mortgage insurance is readily available through banks and insurance companies. Most people consider it normal to get mortgage insurance as soon as they buy a home. The banks readily support that. In fact they'll insist you have insurance because your greatest asset (your home) is collateral on the mortgage.

But the greatest beneficiary of mortgage insurance is the bank. Here's an example:

Let's say you buy a house for $400,000, you put $50,000 down, and get a mortgage for $350,000. Your bank issues you a mortgage insurance policy for the $350,000. Fast forward 10 years, you've now paid down $150,000 but your spouse suddenly passes away. The bank will collect the insurance of $350,000 and pay off your $200,000 mortgage, keeping the balance of $150,000.

You don't have a choice about this. This is how it works. So here's the issue: You may not want to pay off your mortgage, and you may have a greater need for the insurance money to be in your bank account rather than paying your bank.

By receiving the proceeds of the life insurance payout directly you're able to invest the money at perhaps 8% returns while your mortgage interest costs are only 3.5%. It wouldn't make sense in this instance to pay down your mortgage. Furthermore, if the money is invested and available to you, you'd be able to use it for ongoing expenses as needed, or for other things such as a funeral.

Some insurance companies offer mortgage insurance that pays out to you directly as opposed to paying down the mortgage. You have the right to choose whether you use the insurance proceeds to pay your mortgage or not.

Another alternative to mortgage insurance is a general term life insurance policy to cover the mortgage and any final expenses. Eg, couples generally get a Joint First-to-Die policy. This allows the survivor to use the insurance proceeds however makes the most sense. Here's a real life story with fictitious names:

> *Sally and John were happily married with 2 children. John was 37 years old. It had taken me five years of talking about insurance to convince them to get a policy. Within six months of the policy being issued, John was diagnosed with cancer. Within another six months, he passed away. Sally was left with a home, two children and no job. She'd stayed home to raise the kids and therefore had neither a job nor the skills to get one.*
>
> *Because Sally and John had bought a term life policy to cover the mortgage and more, she was able to invest the insurance money and live on it while she upgraded her job skills. She was able to keep her home, and even bought a new van. If Sally had purchased mortgage insurance from the bank, the insurance would have paid for the mortgage but left her nothing as a buffer for the time it took to get back on her feet. She would have had to sell her home and move her children during a very bad time in their lives.*

Assume you own a house. If losing your partner left you mortgage-free but unable to cover your living expenses, then having mortgage insurance may not be your best bet. In this case, you'd be better off with a basic term life policy, where you could invest the insurance payout to provide an ongoing source of income. Otherwise, despite becoming mortgage-free, you could be forced to sell your home to pay for living costs.

Critical illness insurance

With the proliferation of diseases in modern times, critical illness insurance has become more marketable, with many types of policies and payment structures available. This insurance pays out a set amount of money if you're diagnosed with one of the diseases covered by the policy, the most common being heart disease, stroke, Multiple Sclerosis (MS) and cancer. Often a critical illness can be more financially devastating than death. Many require expensive medication and/or medical specialists, increasing the costs to the person who is both ill and unable to work.

As mentioned earlier, stay- at-home moms often require critical illness insurance. The proceeds of this insurance allow you to hire a babysitter or provide child care when Mom is not able.

Most critical Illness policies carry a "return of premiums" option. This means that if, for example, you paid into the policy 10 years but there was no illness, you'd get all of your payments back from the insurer. This sounds like a great plan but you actually pay much higher premiums for this feature. The purpose of insurance is to protect your financial state despite death or illness, not recover your payments because you're lucky to stay healthy!

A key factor in the cost of critical illness insurance is family history. If you have a family history of heart disease, chances are the insurer will "rate" your cost of premiums, meaning you'll pay more for your coverage.

Disability insurance

If you're self-employed, own a business, or run a professional practice, you likely need disability insurance. This insurance will provide you an income if you become injured and unable to work. Various kinds of disability insurance have rating systems related to the occupation being insured. Coverage for a construction worker would be quite different from that of an osteopath.

For example, a specific type of disability insurance is own occupation coverage. This is often used by professionals, eg, doctors, surgeons, therapists, etc, who work with their hands. This means, if they became disabled, they'd be insured until they could resume the job they normally do. Under most general policies, if you become disabled they'll provide an income for a period, but if you can do any other job they deem appropriate, they expect you to do it and get off the disability income. Own occupation disability insurance is expensive but critical for the highly-skilled who aren't willing to do just any job.

Property and casualty insurance

Property and casualty insurance is a "no-brainer". If you have property, protect it against fire, theft and liability. If you rent a property, you only need to cover your personal contents.

People rarely read their property and casualty insurance policies. But it's important, especially with home insurance, to know exactly what's covered. Check for coverage against water damage, usually listed as a separate rider on the policy. Ensure that, if you can't be in your home, the insurance company will pay for a hotel or alternate accommodation.

Check your policy for coverage on theft of jewelry. Generally the maximum coverage is $3,000 unless you add a rider to cover the full value of your jewelry. If you run a business from your home, make sure you have an insurance policy to cover all your business equipment, eg, computers, printers, copiers, phones, etc. Make a list of all items with their serial numbers and perhaps photograph each. Keep this list up to date and store it in a fireproof safe or safety deposit box. This would be needed in case of fire or tragedy to prove the approximate age and value of your business equipment.

Having a knowledgeable insurance broker is a great asset in helping you understand your policies. It's not necessary to be over-insured but basic needs should be met. A good financial planner can help you establish how much insurance you need.

Another useful product is title insurance, which you can purchase after you've paid off your mortgage. Although there are measures in place to prevent people from assuming your property title fraudulently, to be completely reassured, get a lawyer to obtain title insurance on your property. This prevents thieves from stealing your identity and taking out a mortgage on your property that's fully paid off.

Title insurance is also useful when purchasing a resale home. If there are outstanding tax bills or other expenses that weren't caught during the purchase of your new property, title insurance can help pay off these outstanding debts. Your peace of mind is certainly worth the one-time charge of approximately $200 in legal costs. Once you've paid off your mortgage, be sure to get a document from your bank releasing your property and any liens they might have held while you carried a mortgage.

Alternative insurance

Even if you've had a serious illness in the past and aren't eligible for standard types of insurance, you can likely get alternative insurance. Most policies provide a maximum coverage of approximately $25,000 that can be used to cover final expenses. It's expensive but if you can't get insurance on a standard basis, you'd still be eligible for an alternative insurance plan.

Generally it's best to deal with an independent insurance broker who'll shop among various insurance companies to get you the best product at the best price.

Estate planning

Two important objectives in structuring your estate: preserve accumulated capital for your beneficiaries, and minimize taxation at your death. An estate plan enables you to provide sufficient liquidity in your estate so that, after your debts are paid, your remaining assets can be distributed in a timely manner. As much as possible, the estate plan should integrate with your living needs too. No one wants to suffer financially through life in order to be wealthy upon death. At the same time, we all know of family tragedies in which deficient planning contributed to their grief.

Most people don't like to think about dying but, if you think about it sooner than later, you can forget about it for at least five years. If you have a will you should review and update it every five years. If you don't have a will but own property or have children, then shame on you. You must establish power of attorney too. Otherwise, your untimely death could leave your family at risk, holding nothing but a whole pile of headaches.

If you die intestate (without a will), those you've left behind must apply to the courts and government to assume control of your estate. This will take weeks, months and sometimes years of red tape and hassles.

Worse, if you become mentally or physically incapacitated but don't have a power of attorney for your financial affairs, you're putting everything you own at risk. Without a power of attorney, your caregiver(s) can't pay your bills, access your money, or do anything financial on your behalf. If their hands are tied, you could lose property it took years to acquire.

Key considerations in planning your estate are:

- What assets would be kept, and which would be sold?
- How much money do your survivors need upon death, Eg, funeral expenses, to pay off debts, taxes, fund bequests, etc, or provide an education fund for children?
- Is there a need for income? Upon your death, is there anyone for whom you wish to provide an income, and how long should it last?
- Any other needs after your death? Eg, providing eldercare or childcare for a period. How much and how long?
- Any significant purchases or expenses to occur after death? Eg, business buyout, car purchase, different housing needs, etc.

Once you answer these questions, you'll see if your assets are sufficient to meet these needs, or whether you'll need additional capital.

For more helpful details on estate planning, see:
https://joanneshaw.canfin.com/library/category/estate-planning-wills-estate-planning#estate-planning

Wills

A will is a legal declaration directing the disposition of your estate subsequent to your death. It is activated only upon your death, and governs the management of your estate at that time.

Most of us associate a will with images from Hollywood movies - the mourning family huddled together in a lawyer's office, waiting for the surprise announcement that disinherits a once-favored son. In most cases, reality is much less dramatic although I have heard of family cottage fights that went on for many years. Nevertheless, a will is the best way to ensure your wishes are carried out after your death, and an essential element of any estate plan.

If you die intestate (without a will), the courts will decide how your estate will be divided among your family members

This could leave out loved ones and result in delays and a legal and tax bill that's higher than necessary. A legal, up-to-date will makes sure your estate passes smoothly to your beneficiaries. It's the best way to help your family cope during an exceptionally difficult time, and allow them to take advantage of any available tax-saving opportunities.

There are three basic types of will:

- a holograph will is an unwitnessed document entirely in your handwriting and signed by you;
- a form will is one you complete from a do-it-yourself kit; and
- a formal will is drawn up by a professional lawyer or notary.

Note: Both a form will and a formal will must be witnessed by two competent adults who aren't either beneficiaries or the spouses of beneficiaries.

The chief advantage of a formal will is that it's designed to stand up in court under various challenges. It's your lawyer's or notary's responsibility to make sure the wording is absolutely clear and legally binding. When dealing with something as important as your estate, don't leave anything open to interpretation.

Probate fees

Probate is the recognition by the court of the validity of the will and the appointment of the executor or executrix. Your executor must apply for Letters Probate and pay a fee or tax, usually based on the value of your estate assets. Your estate assets are those you hold in sole ownership. Depending on the ownership structure and types of assets you own, your estate may be in a position to avoid probate and its fees.

Some of these fees include:

- Life insurance death benefits where a beneficiary other than the estate is named
- Assets held in registered plans where a living spouse is named as a beneficiary
- Assets held in joint title (tenants in common or with right of survivorship*)
- Assets or income as part of a trust
- Assets of which you are a trustee

"Tenants in common" means you would own a portion of an asset with someone else but that part is yours to sell or pass onto your children, etc, and can't be sold by the person with whom you share ownership. "Joint ownership with rights of survivorship" means that if you die, the jointly held property will immediately become the property of the person with whom you share ownership.

The amount of the probate fee or tax varies between Canadian provinces. For example, in Ontario, typical probate fees are:

- If the value of the estate is less than $50,000, the probate fee will be $5 per $1,000
- If the value of the estate is $50,001 or more the probate fee will be $250 + $15 per $1000 in excess of $50,000

How marriage and divorce affect your will

A will written before your marriage is automatically voided (made invalid) by the act of marriage, unless the will specifically states that it was written in contemplation of your marriage. If your will predates your marriage and was not written in contemplation of it, you're deemed intestate and the provincial intestacy laws would govern the distribution of your estate.

Common-law relationships do not void pre-existing wills.

This means that, if you simply cohabit with someone without marriage, when they die their estate will be distributed according to any will they had prior to your living together, meaning you'd likely receive nothing from his/her estate.

Conversely, If you become divorced, a will prepared prior to your divorce is not automatically revoked. This means that if you divorce and don't update your will, you may leave the people you love out in the cold. However, any assets or bequests left to your ex-spouses are revoked. The appointment of your ex-spouse as your executor is voided and an alternate called upon. All other terms/gifts included in your pre-divorce will are still valid. So if you divorce, prepare a new will.

We all know this story: the woman who moved in with a man who'd previously been married for five years. When he separated from his previous wife, however, he didn't change his will. So when he died 20 years later, the common-law wife who'd lived with him all that time ended up with nothing. The ex-wife got it all because the husband never updated his will. The common-law wife would have a case to present in court for a claim on the estate but this could involve many months and lots of legal bills before anything gets settled.

Don't let this become your story too.

Power of Attorney

A power of attorney for medical care is equally important. If you can't make decisions about your own health care, a power of attorney enables others to give direction to doctors and healthcare workers in your best interests.

A power of attorney (POA) is a legal document, separate from your will that grants another person authority to be your "attorney", to make financial decisions on your behalf when you can't. The POA is in force from the moment you sign it. At your death, the "attorney's" duties end and the executor named in your will take over. You don't need to name the same person as both "attorney" and executor. They're often different.

Powers of attorney can give the other person limited authority to act for you in a specific area or within a specific time, eg, sale of a real estate, or while you're on holiday, in which case it's called a *specific* POA. It can also delegate broader powers, continuing even if you become physically or mentally infirm (in which case it is called an *enduring* POA).

When naming someone as your "attorney," you should also consider an alternate in case your primary "attorney" is unable or unwilling to act in that behalf. Consider someone younger than you. Another option: name your current financial advisor as an expert assistant to the executor. It's a conflict of interest for your financial advisor to be your executor, but they may be listed as an expert financial advisor who can assist in settling the estate.

These "attorney" assignments have far-reaching consequences for which you should obtain appropriate legal counsel.

Once you've established a current will and powers of attorney both financial and medical, you should also consider a pre-arranged funeral.

This relieves your loved ones of making decisions at a time when they're distraught over your demise. You can make choices now to determine what happens once you're gone. Protect your family from the future cost of funerals, whose inflation is almost as bad as education.

For Pre-Arranged funerals: Deal with a reputable company where your money's held in trust by a third party at a guaranteed rate of return. If you're an avid traveler, have a clause in your policy wherein they'll ship your body home from anywhere in the world.

Having an estate plan isn't just for old people. It's essential the moment you own property, have children or get married/live common-law. If you're over 30 and live alone with no property and you don't mind the government getting everything you own, then you can probably get by without a will or powers of attorney. But your surviving family will inherit big headaches.

There are a number of ways in which our best-laid financial plans can become derailed due to death, injury or disability. Having a good estate plan in place with the appropriate documents, and having the appropriate amount of insurance coverage for your needs, is critical to maintaining a strong financial position. By being proactive in the area of estate planning and insurance, you can avoid potential financial disasters in the future.

One of the ways in which we can avoid financial headaches is to be defensive in our financial affairs. This involves proactive saving, protecting your family and ensuring you can purchase and sustain the major items you need in life.

Next, let's look at how to be financially defensive!

CHAPTER 4: DEFENCE

It's important to be aware of your financial situation by tracking income and spending. It's smart to protect yourself from disaster by insuring against accident, illness or death. But neither are enough to guarantee a comfortable retirement.

For that, you need a strategy – to grow your assets while guarding them from loss. The first goal of the game plan is to accumulate wealth.

There's a mantra in my business:

PAY YOURSELF FIRST!

Have you ever noticed that once you commit to regularly paying "X" dollars towards something, eventually you don't even notice the money leaving your account? That's what paying yourself first is all about. An automatic monthly contribution to savings which fits your budget will ensure that your investments will grow and compound over time.

I have a client who could only afford to save $25 a month for her children's education. Although her kids are still years away from needing the money, she's accumulated over $6,000.

A leaky tap fills a barrel one drip at a time. Just make sure the drip is in your favor.

Time is an important factor in saving money. The sooner you start the better. A 20-year-old who invests $5,000 has years for it to collect and compound returns. Given the right assets and enough time, it could turn into hundreds of thousands of dollars.

Remember: you're in charge of your own financial security, not the government, your employer, your partner or your kids. It's up to you, so start today. Give up cigarettes or some other indulgence. Put the money into a mutual fund. You'll be amazed at how fast it can grow.

It's also important to defend yourself against inadequate information, bad advice or unnecessary hardship. For example, the biggest expense of your life will likely be a home. Do you know what it takes to qualify for a mortgage?

Years ago there weren't many options for getting a mortgage. Most people immediately thought of a bank. Today there are more options. A mortgage broker can search for the best rates from various lenders. The broker can also find the best mortgage for your needs. First let's see what it takes to qualify.

How to qualify for a mortgage

Your income, versus current and ongoing expenses, is key to qualifying for a mortgage. Generally you need to keep your accommodation expenses within a certain percentage of your income. Exceed that limit through high condo fees or credit card debt and you may find yourself with a house but no mortgage to cover it. If you failed to have a plan for obtaining a mortgage and you lost your dream home, this would be an example of an unnecessary hardship.

To understand how to qualify for a mortgage, consider these two terms: Gross Debt Service Ratio (GDSR) and Total Debt Service Ratio (TDSR)

What are GDSR and TDSR?

When you apply for a mortgage, the mortgage broker asks the immediate questions:

1. What's your gross family income, and where does it come from?
2. What are your payments to credit cards, loans, leases, alimony and child support?
3. What's the price of the property, condo fees if any, and current property taxes?

This information is necessary to assess your ability to carry the mortgage you want. Lending institutions that offer mortgages use two ratios to determine that ability. One is the Gross Debt Service Ratio (GDSR), the other the Total Debt Service Ratio (TDSR).

GDSR: Gross Debt Service Ratio

GDSR is the percentage of your gross income (32%) that can be used to pay mortgage debt, property taxes, 50% of your condo fees, and heat allocation (very important in Canada). Here's a typical scenario:

$60,000 gross annual income = $5000 a month X 32% = $1,600 a month (housing allowance)

Monthly expenses: $75 heat + $230 property taxes + (50% of $500 = $250) condo fees = $555 / month

$1,600 housing allowance - $555 monthly expenses = **$1045** left for mortgage payments

With that combination of income and expenses, you'd qualify to buy a home of approximately $234,342, assuming a (current) 3.5% interest rate and 25-year amortization.

If you had no condo fees this would reduce your expenses and make more of your money available for a mortgage: $1,600 income - $75 heat -$230 taxes = **$1295** per month.

TDSR: Total Debt Service Ratio

TDSR is the percentage of your gross income (40%) that can be used to pay mortgage debt, property taxes, 50% of your condo fees, an allocation towards heat and all other payments outside of accommodation to which you are committed.

Outside committed payments would include:

- car loans

- student loan payments
- leases
- credit card payments
- lines of credit/loans
- alimony/child support payments
- personal guarantees on other person's loans

Here's another typical scenario:

$60,000 gross annual income = $5000 per month X 40% = $2000 per month

Monthly expenses: $75 heat + $230 taxes + $250 condo fees + $300 all monthly committed payments (ACP) = $855 / month

$2,000 expense allowance - $855 monthly expenses = **$1145** left for mortgage payments

If you had no condo fees this would reduce your expenses and make more of your money available for a mortgage: $2,000 income - $75 heat -$230 taxes- $300 (ACP) = **$1395** per month

As you can see, the size of your debt, the amount of property taxes, and whether or not you have condo fees, is critical in determining your ability to carry a mortgage.

In the excitement of finding the home of your dreams, this is likely the last thing on your mind. To purchase a home you must know exactly what you can afford. This proactive defence strategy gives you the tools you need to determine what mortgage you can handle for the best home you can afford.

Other defensive actions in home buying

- ✓ Check your own credit rating or beacon score (available through Equifax) in advance to ensure you're not listed with an ongoing debt that doesn't exist. Ensure that all the information in your file is correct.
- ✓ Avoid posted rates for mortgages. Posted rates are the listing of interest rates currently offered by the financial institution. These are the highest possible interest rates available.
- ✓ Avoid visiting many institutions for quotes. Each time someone searches your credit score, it negatively affects it. You can avoid this by working with a broker who'll search various lenders on your behalf with little or no effect on your credit score.
- ✓ Check the details of the home you plan to buy. Most property sellers don't mind providing details like heating and water costs. The real estate listing generally shows the annual property taxes on the property fact sheet. Condo fees should be provided too.
- ✓ Falsifying documents to secure a mortgage is a criminal offence. If anyone suggests you do that, drop them immediately and consider reporting them.
- ✓ Stay as close to your budget as possible and keep in mind you'll incur various other expenses once you buy. Prepare an advanced estimate of costs, eg, legal fees, moving costs, inspection fees, closing costs. If you're selling your current home and moving, you'll have additional fees like final taxes, real estate commission, appraisal costs, etc.

- ✓ Make a conditional offer on the home you want to purchase. This allows you to get an inspection done and set up your finances for the mortgage (get a written pre-approval if possible). Read the fine print of any exclusion so that you don't take possession expecting a washer and dryer when they were actually listed in the contract as *not* part of the house sale.
- ✓ When taking out a mortgage or other substantial debt, the interest rate is a major factor. A one-percent saving on a mortgage (or other large debt) reduces by an enormous amount the interest payments over the life of any long-term debt. Be sure you understand the real interest rate on your debts - not just the posted rate. More frequent compounding of interest (eg, "daily compounding" charged by department store credit cards) can increase the effective interest rate from the 24% that is posted to an actual 27.1% per year. Always try to pay off the most expensive, non-tax-deductible debts first.
- ✓ If you've saved money in your RRSP and you don't plan to retire for several years, you can use the Home Buyers Plan (HBP) to make a down payment on your first home and, under some conditions, perhaps use it again. (Do the research or consult your financial advisor.) You're allowed to borrow the money from your RRSP, paying neither withholding tax nor interest. You have 15 years to pay back the "loan" from your RRSP and are expected to payback 1/15th of the amount each year by contribution to your RRSP. If you don't put the money back into your RRSP on schedule, the amount of the missed repayment is added to

your income for that year. The RRSP contribution room can't be recouped.

- ✓ If you go with a variable rate mortgage please, never lock it in unless interest rates begin to skyrocket overnight. When you lock in a variable-rate mortgage it's always done at the posted rate – the highest possible interest rate on a mortgage. If you get nervous about such things, stick with a fixed rate mortgage and you'll sleep better.
- ✓ Budget for home maintenance. The age of the home will determine the budget. When you buy a resale home you should have acquired full disclosure of any potential maintenance issues. Even if your home is brand new and needs no maintenance, you should budget for redecorating and new furniture.

The next big expenditure is a car

Next to buying a home, the most expensive item for most of us is a car. There are so many variables in a car purchase it's difficult to state the general rules. The average buyer either pays in cash or buys on credit. The simplest way to buy a car is to save up the money, go to a dealership and pick out your car.

Most people manage to buy a car no matter how bad their credit rating. Lots of small car dealers will offer financing regardless of your credit. Either the car dealer or the trust company behind the dealership will provide a loan with a set term and interest rate. But beware of the interest rate you'll pay. Before signing a contract check the interest rate and the compounding of interest (monthly or annual) where annual is preferred. You may want to check other sources to see if you can get a loan at a better rate.

The cost of car ownership isn't limited to purchase price. There's also maintenance to keep it in good running order, and normal operating costs, eg, licensing, insurance and fuel. These ongoing costs must be factored into your budget.

Let's begin by determining what kind of car you want, or need? What it will cost you? For their first vehicle, many people buy a used car because they can't afford a new one. The plus side of buying a used car is that your car will not depreciate immediately upon sale as happens with a new car. As soon as you drive a new car off the dealership lot, it loses value.

The internet is a great source of information on types and prices of cars. Go to dealerships and see what's for sale and what they cost. Dealerships generally have both new and previously owned (used) cars. Look in the newspaper's classified section or on the internet and see how much private sellers are asking for the car you want. Be especially careful in buying a used car.

Before going to a dealership or a private seller, research the model, year and current prices for the car of your dreams. This will give you an advantage when negotiating a sale. This will also help you make an educated decision about price, colour, extras, etc. Other items to research are "lemons", ie, cars that are no good, and "black book" value, ie, the typical depreciated value of used cars. Banks use the black book value to determine the amount of collateral the car will secure.

Quick tips when buying a used car

1. Buy from a reliable, well-established dealer
2. Always ask why the car is being sold, or why it was sold to the dealership
3. Find out how many miles/kilometres are on the car (average use is 20,000 km/year)
4. Always have an independent mechanic check the car for reliability
5. Ask for the maintenance history of the car and get the written records if possible
6. Check to make sure that you won't have any major expenses, eg, new tires, brakes, battery or major repairs that add to your immediate cost. Tires should last 60,000-100,000 km. Some batteries last the life of the car, but brakes need to be maintained and checked regularly.
7. Confirm whether the car has had any special coatings to prevent rust
8. Confirm the type of fuel and the mileage that the car gets
9. Always negotiate the price
10. If you must finance the car, ask what interest rates the dealership will charge, and compare their rate to a bank car loan or line of credit. In particular, check how interest is compounded on the loan. Annual is better than monthly.
11. Ask if there's any existing warranty and how long it will last

Instead of borrowing money to buy a car, the best way is to save up the money and pay in cash. Let's say you want to buy a car in five years. If the car costs $15,000, you'll have to save $3,000 a year for five years. That means saving $250 a month or $62.50 a week.

Buying is just the initial investment. You must also plan for all the other expenses involved in maintaining and operating your car. The following are examples of some ongoing costs:

1. Vehicle registration license - approximately $100 a year
2. Taxes on the sale of the vehicle - depends where it's purchased but approximately 13% (on a $15,000 car, that's $1,950). This is a one-time fee so if we add tax you'd need to save $70.63 a week for five years to afford it.
3. Insurance for the car - $1250 a year depending on driver's age and driving record
4. Fuel costs - $60 to $100 a week depending on how much driving
5. Annual oil changes and maintenance - budget $500 a year for a new car, $1,000 for a car less than five years old, and $1,500+ for a car over five years old.
6. Emission testing - another expense based on the age of the car. (Approximately $40)

Although you pay for your personal driver's license when you pass your test, you must renew your driving license every five years, the fee for which is approximately $100.

One final thing to do when you buy a car: take it to a dealership or reliable mechanic to get it checked out. Dealerships are generally more expensive because of overhead and the mechanics' higher rate of pay. With some cars it may be better to use the dealership because you want to make sure they have the correct parts for the car. The most important thing is to know your car and maintain it accordingly. The more cars you own, the more educated you become in the process of buying and selling cars.

Love, common-law, marriage and divorce

We can't discuss money and finance without addressing the possibility of marriage and separation. Nothing devastates a financial plan faster than divorce or separation.

Since love seems to have a negative effect on our ability to think rationally, many people have suffered as a consequence. Therefore, be cautious with regard to the following scenarios:

1. If you're the principal holder of a credit card and you add your partner's name to that credit card, ***you're still the only one liable***. So if your new partner racks up $60,000 on your credit card, you have to pay it. You can't take their name off the card or cancel it until you've paid off the balance. She/he can walk away from the debt, but you can't.
2. If you and your new partner intend to buy property together, try to secure an equal financial contribution to its purchase. If you put up all the money, don't put your partner's name on the title deed (the title deed states who owns the property). If you're the sole owner and you break up within three years, your partner could fight for some compensation but isn't likely to

be successful. But if you stay together for more than three years (even if common-law) half of the property will go to your partner.

One exception: If you were previously married and your will bequeathed everything to your ex-partner, if you did not update your will, when you die your property will go to your ex (as per certain regulations). Your current partner could take it to court to gain compensation but this could become very costly. Keep in mind this could work against you if the roles were reversed.

Although choosing to marry or live common-law is a personal decision, be aware of the consequences from a tax and property perspective. It's particularly important for single mothers, a subject we'll return to when we discuss taxes.

Separation and divorce are huge topics whose ramifications go beyond the scope of this book but we can cover some key issues:

1. If you're thinking of separating, speak with either a family/divorce lawyer or a divorce mediator. They can help you determine reasonable expectations in the division of property, especially when it comes to custody cases. A good divorce mediator is worth consulting, because they can help to reduce court time and legal costs.
2. In Ontario, the moment you cease living together you're considered legally separated. There may not be a separation of assets as yet,

but for tax and other purposes this is considered the date of separation.

3. When children are involved, be an adult and spare your children's suffering due to your personal anger and discontent with your ex-partner. Your kids didn't choose to be born or live in this situation. For their sake, stay on reasonable terms with your ex where possible. Keep this in mind when it comes to custody and visitation. Unless your ex is abusive, everyone has a right to see their own children. If they're abusive, that's another matter, and then you need to fight to protect your kids. But if you falsely accuse your ex of abuse, you should go to jail. False accusations make it that much harder to verify when actual abuse is going on. This is doubly devastating for a family.

4. If you expect to receive child support, you must file a document with the courts outlining details of such support. If the support isn't forthcoming, the Family Responsibility Office (FRO) can help in securing these payments. This government organization has the power, if support payments aren't made, to deny the renewal of driver's licences and passports. Jail time is also a possibility.

Personally, I feel I've had both a terrible marriage and a great one (although not to the same person), so I have a few insights into what makes a solid marriage. When I was called upon recently to give a speech, my topic was "Love, Marriage and Divorce". See Appendix 3 for my checklist for a good marriage.

Credit, Debit and Points

Although it's pervasive in our society, plastic money is just that - plastic. It's not real. A great deal of modern society's debt problems could probably be eased by a return to real cash. In particular, university students and first-time wage-earners seem to have the impression that a credit card means real money. It doesn't. When the credit card bill comes in, you need real money to pay it off! That sounds simple but we've all heard, "Oh, I can buy that, I have a credit card!" At which point I say, how will you pay for it? "Oh, I have a credit card!" and we go around in circles.

On a personal note, I've never paid interest on a credit card, never had an NSF (non-sufficient funds) cheque, and have never used the overdraft protection on my bank account. I'm not bragging, just stating a fact, because it's not pride, it's common sense. These are just forms of temporary or emergency funding - nice to have but not to be used unless you're desperate.

When you buy things with a credit card, you need to know that the money to pay off the credit card is either already in the bank or will be by the time you receive your bill. It's as simple as that. Don't cultivate an "out of sight, out of mind" mentality, wherein the card makes the purchase but somehow you don't foresee the need for money to pay the inevitable bill at the end of the month, and so you can kind of forget about it. ..

I'm not a fan of credit cards but there's one use of points which is great. With some credit cards, you can apply points received to pay down your line of credit (LOC). Now there's a good use of points.

In terms of your debit card, follow these precautions:

- Never give your PIN (personal identification number) to anyone. This is very important if you ever have a security breach. The banks will support you so long as you haven't shared your PIN with anyone. Generally they'll reverse any unknown or wrongly-sourced purchases.
- Always block the view of your hand area while entering your PIN into an ATM machine or in any store's card reader. Keep your debit card in sight to avoid double swiping.
- Keep your debit card in a safe place, preferably out of sight in a compartment of your wallet.
- If you need someone else to access your funds and pay bills, for example, while you're travelling, write up a power-of-attorney or open a joint account so they can make financial decisions in your absence. This should be someone you know so well you can trust them with your money.

Bad Credit

Many things can negatively affect your credit rating. Some people lack guidance and education. If your credit is bad, you need to fix it. That may require filing for bankruptcy or a consumer proposal. A consumer proposal enables you to restructure your debt and pay it off in accordance to what you can afford over a period of time.

Since it will take seven years to clear your credit after bankruptcy, this is a forced return to cash. You can buy a credit card up front and use this to rebuild your credit rating. For example, you can pay a credit card company $500 and they'll give you a credit card for that amount. Now you've paid up-front, and each purchase with the card draws from that balance. Eventually, this helps to re-establish your credit rating.

Investments

Investment is the action or process of investing money for profit or material result.

Risk and Asset Allocation

Asset allocation is a way to understand and manage your investments better by dividing your portfolio into different kinds of assets. This is known as diversification or having your eggs in different baskets, eg, cash, stocks, bonds and real estate. Your portfolio allocation should reflect your investor personality. The investor personality profile reflects your personality as it relates to your tolerance for risk, need for liquidity, and the timeline for reaching goals.

Investing your hard-earned financial resources can bring both benefits and risk. But there is a balance that must be reached between the potential return of an investment and the risk associated with that investment.

You should never accept more risk than you are comfortable with. ***Choose a level of risk that lets you sleep at night without concern and anxiety.***

The chart below outlines the various categories of investments and the risks associated with them. Each area of investment has a specific volatility in the marketplace. The amount of risk involved depends upon the ups and downs for that particular investment. Although you can buy an investment that might return 35%, that same investment is just as likely to lose 35%. And that's where you begin to lose sleep. If you can't tolerate this magnitude of market swings, you need a more conservative investment.

Investing is a very personal thing. The way you want to invest may not match your partner's idea of investing. When it comes to couples, you may have the same timeframe and objectives as your partner but you may have a very different risk tolerance. This means a different approach to investing, particularly for jointly held accounts. Don't let anyone else dictate your risk tolerance. I've had to fire clients because the husband insisted that his wife be invested according to *his* risk tolerance. It's against regulations and it's against good sense.

Asset Allocation Categories

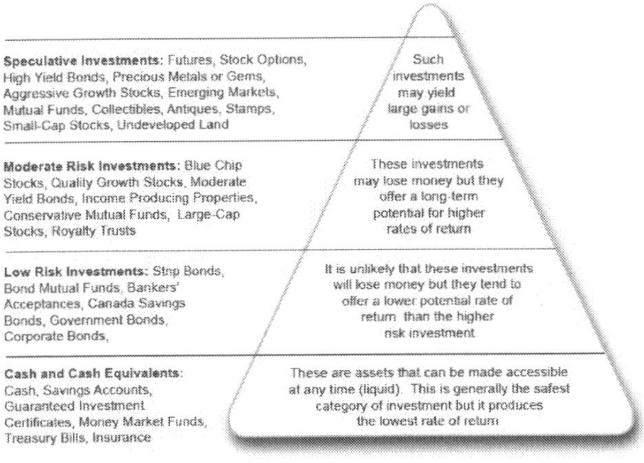

The Investor Education Fund helps people make effective use of financial information. The Investor Education Fund was established by the Ontario Securities Commission, the province's securities regulator, and is funded by OSC enforcement settlements. It operates separately from the OSC with its own Board of Directors.

There's a saying in my business: *"Two things will destroy an investor – fear and greed."*

It's important to invest according to your own personal risk tolerance level but beware as well of being too cautious. Many people are so afraid of investing that everything they own is in a savings account or GICs. The problem with being too risk adverse is that you may end up making negative returns. If you're in GICs, you may be making minus three percent on your investments. How do I come to this conclusion?

Interest income earned on GICs is taxable in the year in which it occurs. You're taxed at the highest possible rate (marginal tax rate) on GICs. And if you're lucky, they're paying 2%. But after inflation (3%) and your marginal tax rate (35-46% in some cases) you end up paying more in taxes and taking less in returns, thus a negative return.

On the flip side, some investors are too greedy. They're constantly looking for the magic formula to get rich quick. This creates two problems. First, they're vulnerable to "get-rich-quick" scams. Second, they're never happy with a normal, manageable rate of return over time. So beware: if the returns on an investment sound too good to be true, then they probably are just that - too good to be true. Walk away.

The solution is a balanced approach to investing that will give you the security you need and still allow you to sleep soundly at night. In my experience, the more educated the investor, the more balanced things are for that client. They're invested properly to achieve their goals in a manageable time frame with a reasonable amount of risk. And, most important, they can sleep at night without worrying about their life savings.

If you wish to test your own risk level, you can find a number of different risk tolerance questionnaires online. A Certified Financial Planner (CFP) has an obligation to ensure that you're properly invested according to your risk tolerance, your investment objectives and your timeframe.

Investment Vehicles

There are many ways to buy into the markets and many ways in which your money may be held at an investment institution. Most people are familiar with the concept of stocks and mutual funds, but there are a variety of accounts which may hold these various investments classes. I call these "Umbrella" vehicles - an RRSP, RRIF, RESP, RDSP, TFSA, etc - where a mutual fund, GIC, stock or bond may be managed under that umbrella.

We have the privilege in Canada where several investment vehicles are supported by government grants and bonds, or tax advantages. The RRSP, RRIF, RESP, RDSP and TFSA are all fairly unique to Canada. Canada's system of offering tax deductions and tax credits is a very robust system shared with only a few other countries in the world. For this reason alone it's to your benefit to take advantage of them to invest and receive immediate compensation in the form of grants, tax deductions, and tax deferral. Following is a general description of the most common investment vehicles.

RRSP: Registered Retirement Savings Plan

The Government of Canada introduced the RRSP to encourage Canadians to save for their own retirement, or at least supplement their Canadian Pension Plan (CPP) benefits. Every dollar you invest in an RRSP while working is a dollar deducted from this year's taxable income. When you retire, your withdrawals from your RRSP become taxable income, but presumably at a lower tax bracket since you will be in retirement and drawing less income than when you were working.

When Canada first came out with the CPP, the average mortality rate of the day was age 67 for men and 70 for women. Today we are living much longer; thus the RRSP becomes an even more critical source of retirement funding.

There are limits on how much you can put into your RRSP each year. This is determined by a percentage of your gross income for the prior tax year. Eg, if you made $40,000 in 2017, the maximum contribution to your RRSP for 2018 would be: $40,000 X 18% = $7,200.

There's a ceiling for people in high income brackets wherein their RRSP contribution is limited. This is a set amount as opposed to a percentage, and these amounts may vary from year to year. The current 18% rule may be changed by the government at their discretion.

If you have unused room for RRSP contribution, you may be able to add more to your RRSP in that year. But if you over-contribute by more than $2,000, you'll be subject to penalty fees from the Canadian Customs and Revenue Agency (CCRA).

RRIF: Registered Retirement Income Fund

At a specific age (currently age 71) the Government will require you to convert all RRSP holdings to a RRIF. There's a set percentage that may change year to year but generally you have a choice of either a maximum or minimum withdrawal amount. Where possible, always pick the minimum. You can always increase the withdrawal amount as needed. Since the minimum withdrawal is generally 5-5.5% of your total portfolio, it's important to prepare in advance for this conversion from RRSP to RRIF.

You must be aware of how this will affect your income. If you converted a $500,000 portfolio to a RRIF, at 5.5% you'd be required to withdraw $27,500 annually. If you're already receiving a company pension, CPP and perhaps OAS, this will definitely bump you into a higher tax bracket. One way to prevent this is to begin "downsizing" your RRSP portfolio before you reach age 71. This way, you can withdraw money at the lowest possible tax rate (assuming you've stopped working) and re-invest in a different vehicle such as a TFSA or non-registered (Open) investment. This reduces the amount you'll be required to withdraw from your RRIF, thus reducing your overall income tax.

TFSA: Tax Free Savings Account

The Tax-Free Savings Account (TFSA) is a flexible, registered, general-purpose savings vehicle that allows Canadians to earn tax-free investment income to more easily meet lifetime savings needs. The TFSA complements existing registered savings plans like the Registered Retirement Savings Plans (RRSP) and the Registered Education Savings Plans (RESP).

The TFSA limit determines how much you can deposit in your Tax-Free Savings Account each year. The TFSA limit for 2018:

Year	TFSA Annual Limit	TFSA Cumulative Limit
2009	$5,000	$5,000
2010	$5,000	$10,000
2011	$5,000	$15,000
2012	$5,000	$20,000
2013	$5,500	$25,500
2014	$5,500	$31,000
2015	$10,000	$41,000
2016	$5,500	$46,500
2017	$5,500	$52,000
2018	$5,500	$57,500

How the TFSA works:

- As of January 1, 2013, Canadian residents age 18 and older can contribute up to $5,500 annually to a TFSA. This is an increase from the annual contribution limit of $5,000 for 2009 through 2012 and reflects indexation to inflation.
- Investment income earned in a TFSA is tax-free.
- Withdrawals from a TFSA are tax-free.
- Unused TFSA contribution room is carried forward and accumulates in future years.
- Full amount of withdrawals can be put back into the TFSA in future years. Re-contributing in the same year may result in an over-contribution subject to a penalty tax.

- You can choose from a wide range of investment options such as mutual funds, GICs and bonds.
- Contributions are not tax-deductible.
- Neither income earned within a TFSA nor withdrawals from it affect eligibility for federal income-tested benefits and credits, such as Old Age Security, the Guaranteed Income Supplement, and the Canada Child Tax Benefit.
- Funds can be given to a spouse or common-law partner for them to invest in their TFSA.
- TFSA assets can generally be transferred to a spouse or common-law partner upon death. You may also designate a Successor for your TFSA account in the case of your death.

What are the differences between a TFSA and an RRSP?

- ✓ An RRSP is primarily intended for retirement savings. Tax assistance provided by a TFSA complements that provided through RRSPs.
- ✓ RRSP contributions are tax-deductible, while RRSP withdrawals are added to income and taxed at regular rates.
- ✓ TFSA contributions are not tax-deductible, but the contributions and the investment earnings are exempt from tax upon withdrawal.
- ✓ Unlike an RRSP, which must be converted to a retirement income vehicle at age 71, a TFSA does not have any minimum withdrawal requirement.
- ✓ There is no TFSA spousal plan. Individuals can provide funds to their spouse or common-law partner to invest in their TFSA, up to the spouse's or common-law partner's available

room, and the income earned on the contributed amount is generally not attributed back to the spouse or partner who provided the funds. *(Attribution laws affect the investment of funds between partners and have a specific effect on taxes and how they're applied to the investments.)*

Saving for your children's education

What's the link between education and earnings? A recent report (*Education at a Glance 2009,* Paris: OECD, 2009, p. 137) confirms that, with few exceptions, earnings increase with each level of education. The earnings benefit of higher education can be explained as follows:

In Canada, people with a university degree (Bachelor, Masters, or Doctorate) earned $171 for every $100 earned by high-school graduates. Those with a college degree earned $111 for every $100 earned by high-school graduates. Those who didn't graduate from high school earned only $75 for every $100 earned by high-school grads.

Education is seen as the most desirable route to earning a decent living and to enhancing personal growth and happiness. Educated people not only earn higher incomes but also contribute disproportionally to business innovation, productivity, and national economic performance. There is a strong and direct relationship between investments in education, educational attainment, and economic growth. Recent evidence also suggests that educated people make decisions that lead to healthier and longer lives.

Education drives success.

Given the increasing cost of post-secondary education, saving for your children's education is critical. The two most popular options are ITF accounts and RESPs.

ITF accounts

As minors can't hold investments in their own names, parents commonly establish education savings accounts in trust for them. While not formal trusts, these "in trust for" (ITF) accounts operate as though they were irrevocable trusts just the same. The observance of these rules ensures that any capital gains arising from the investments are taxed in the hands of the minor child and, as long as the amount of taxable capital gains is not significant, there won't be any tax due from this income. There are no limits on the amount that can be invested nor are there any restrictions on what the funds are used for as long as they are intended for the beneficiary.

Registered Education Savings Plans (RESPs)

Parents may wish to invest in an RESP. This defers any income taxes on growth and income within the plan, making it taxable in the hands of the child as they attend a post-secondary educational institution. There's no deduction from income as there is with the RRSP. The maximum lifetime contribution per child is $50,000. In addition, based on your annual family income the federal government offers a 20%, 30% or 40% matching grant (Canada Education Savings Grant (CESG)) ranging from $500 to $600 per child per year up to a total grant of $7,200 over the lifetime of the plan.

If none of the named beneficiaries pursues a post-secondary education, the contributions can be redeemed by the parent tax-free. The total amount of the government grant excluding the growth associated with these funds must be paid back to the government. The remaining balance, the growth on the contributions in the plan, can be withdrawn and invested into the contributor's RRSP (as long as there is contribution room). If there is no room available, the withdrawn money will be taxed in the hands of the contributor at their marginal tax rate plus an additional 20% tax (12% in Quebec).

You can contribute to an RESP each year up to and including the year your child reaches age 17. Contributions for children 16 and 17 are eligible for government grants only if contributions of at least $100 per year were made in any four years before the child reaches age 16, or a minimum of $2,500 has been contributed before the year in which the child reaches age 16. It's also possible to contribute two years at a time on a carry-forward basis so that if you couldn't contribute to an RESP one year, you can double up the following year.

RDSP: Registered Disability Savings Plan

The RSDP was introduced in 2008 by the Government of Canada to provide a vehicle for families in which a member has a disability. In general families and their loved ones with disabilities face unique financial challenges. The RDSP was designed to provide assisted savings and tax-deferred investment growth. Following are the current qualifying criteria:

- You must be a citizen of Canada
- You must be eligible for the Disability Tax Credit
- You must be less than 60 years of age (Note: most assisted savings don't apply after age 49)
- You must have a valid Social Insurance Number (SIN)

The Government offers various grants and bonds to augment individual contributions to the plan. Part of the criteria for the amount received is based on family income. The maximum lifetime contribution is $200,000, with no annual limits on how much you can contribute. An important feature of the RDSP is that it's possible to transfer funds, eg, from a deceased parent's RRSP or RRIF, to a child with disabilities. An RDSP is limited as to eligible types of investments. The RDSP is fairly complex relative to how grants and bonds are provided. If you think you need an RDSP, talk to your financial planner.

Inside the investment vehicle

Within an RRSP, RRIF or TFSA, etc, you may hold stocks, mutual funds, GICs and bonds.

Stocks

A stock is a direct investment into a publicly-traded company. Since you need to go through a stockbroker, for each purchase or sale of stock you'll pay a commission fee. Each stock differs in risk. Eg, investing in a well-established corporate utility like Bell Canada isn't the same as buying a penny stock where the risk is very high. Note that, when dealing with a stockbroker, you're required to sign a limited power of attorney agreement. This gives your stockbroker the power to buy and sell stocks on your behalf. When you hear of a major scam where someone ran off with a client's life savings, it's usually because the money manager had the power to access and transfer money without the client's signature. If you want to invest in stocks, make sure you have the time, knowledge and patience to understand the markets and keep close watch on your investments.

Mutual Funds

A mutual fund is a pooled investment from many investors who share a common money manager. This has a number of positive effects. The cost of transactions, the fees of the actual fund manager, and various costs such as legal, administrative, etc, are drastically reduced compared to buying the investments directly. The other bonus is that you receive high level management of your money by a fund manager who is expert in that area. One example would be a mutual fund investing in Asian businesses where the fund manager would actually be located in Asia and thus have first-hand knowledge of local economic conditions and industry activity. Money managers make the buying and selling decisions for the mutual fund. They generally have a team of researchers that follow the various companies that the fund manager is interested in. This same team provides timely information on when to buy or sell equities.

The relative safety of a mutual fund is that all risks are spread among a number of investors, as well as among various holdings within the fund. An example would be a fund holding corporate stocks, eg, Bell, Apple, etc, as well as fixed income products such as Government of Canada bonds. Such mutual funds enable you to take a balanced approach to investing.

Each mutual fund is limited to a 10% maximum holding of any individual stock or bond. This is a form of protection too. Nortel was a rude wake-up call because the stock price had been quite high for years and suddenly fell drastically to a point of almost no value. If you'd been holding Nortel stock directly, you would've lost it all. But if held in a mutual fund, your maximum exposure would have been only 10% of the fund's overall holdings.

Mutual funds are available in different investment categories, each with differing levels of risk. A general Asian fund would invest in Asian businesses but it could also specifically target Japan or India. As a general rule, the more specific the fund, the greater your risk when all your eggs are in one basket. The more you diversify your investments, the more you spread your risk.

Although there are economies that are more stable than others for ex, Canada's market is generally more stable than the market in a country such as Brazil, we live in a global economy so any major event in the world can have an impact on all markets.

When dealing with banks or other investment providers, be aware that many offer their own brand of mutual funds. But it's important to remember, you want unbiased investment advice. If I work for a bank that offers their own mutual funds, you can bet they'll want me to promote their brand. In some cases I may be compensated more for selling what the company wants me to sell. From an investment standpoint, this isn't a very objective approach to meeting *your* needs.

Guaranteed Investment Certificate (GIC)

A GIC is a product that pays a lower rate of return in exchange for guaranteeing that your money will be there when you want it. The current rate for GICs is 1-3%. What's really happening with a GIC is that the institution you buy it from pays you a 2% return, meanwhile reinvesting the money to make 8-10% or more.

GICs serve a purpose for people with limited income, eg, seniors and retirees, or someone wanting to park their money for less than three years. It's not appropriate for a 35-year-old guy, a 40-something single mom or anyone who has a reasonable time to invest. It's usually fear or lack of knowledge that gets people invested in GICs. You may invest in GICs because that's what your parents did. But things have changed.

There are many good alternatives to GIC investing which provide a balanced rate of return without high risk. A fixed income mutual fund is an example of an investment which is conservative, low risk and yet has the potential to earn 4-6% returns.

Bonds

Bonds are used to finance a certificate issued by a government or corporation promising to pay back borrowed money at a fixed rate of interest on a specified date. Think of Canada Savings Bonds and you'll get the idea. There are long-term bonds and short-term bonds. The choice of which to buy and when varies with current economic conditions, your time frame and your goal for the investment. You can hold bonds within a mutual fund. But if you purchase bonds directly, you'll again need a bond trader or stockbroker.

Miscellaneous Definitions

Following are some other investment programs and vehicles that you may encounter.

Home Buyers Plan (HBP)

The HBP allows you to borrow from your RRSP, tax-free and interest-free. There are specific criteria and dollar limits. You have 15 years to pay back the loan, repaying 1/15th of the borrowed amount each year, or else have that amount added to that year's taxable income.

Life Long Learning Plan (LLP)

The LLP facilitates funding your education for any qualified course with a 10-year interest-free loan. This is another opportunity to use your RRSP for tax-free interest-free advantage. You borrow money from your own RRSP to pay for schooling, then repay 1/10th a year or else the money is added to that year's taxable income.

Segregated Funds

A segregated fund is an insurance product offering a guarantee. It's popular with seniors because the money's invested in the market but the principal (original amount) is guaranteed. There's a minimum holding period for these investments, usually 10 years. The insurance company is betting on the expectation that any decent investment will do well at some point over a 10-year period. These funds can only be purchased from a licensed insurance salesperson. The downside of segregated funds is that the fund-management costs aren't transparent. Furthermore, by locking your money into a specific fund for 10 years you might miss out on other investment opportunities.

Taxation

There are two inevitable things in life - death and taxes. When you die the Canadian Revenue Agency requires two tax returns: a final and a terminal tax return. There's no way to escape taxes.

First, let us make a distinction between tax evasion and tax avoidance. Tax evasion is a criminal offense. Tax avoidance is legal and encouraged. The Canadian tax system is an honour system whereby the tax payer submits details of their own income, taxes paid, tax credits and eligible deductions, and the government checks the information for validity.

Whether or not you file income tax is based upon your residency (where you live). If you're a Canadian citizen living in Canada and receiving income from another country then you have to claim this income on your Canadian tax return as worldwide income. But a Canadian citizen working overseas or in the USA will file the appropriate taxes for where they are living. This is very different from a USA citizen who is required to file a US tax return regardless of where in the world they are living.

It's quite common for a Canadian citizen working in the USA to still have an RRSP in Canada. But they will have to declare their holdings to the US government. A Canadian RRSP is not subject to USA tax laws however, if you're a US citizen in Canada and own a TFSA account, the US government will still tax you on this "tax-free" account.

Of all expenses shown on your cash flow, income tax is usually the largest. Unfortunately, the majority of us don't understand how this is calculated, what measures can reduce it, or how to restructure and/or defer the receipt of income until future years when we may be in a lower tax bracket.

The most important tax concept to understand is "marginal tax rate," the percentage of tax you pay on the last dollar of income you earn. It's the rate that applies to tax deferral and tax deductions. For most people, the first priority in reducing their tax bill should be to make RRSP contributions. Not only do RRSPs give you a tax deduction equal to your marginal tax rate, but they also allow the invested funds to grow without paying tax on the annual return. This is the most beneficial part of RRSPs.

In addition to maximizing tax deductions, you should try to maximize tax credits. Tax credits are available for low-income spouses, persons with disabilities, education expenses such as tuition fees, pension income, medical expenses, and charitable donations, to name just a few. Much has been written about other tax strategies, tax planning techniques, and ways to effectively avoid and/or minimize tax. At this point, any strategy that is designed simply and solely to save tax will likely fail. Unless the investment that is designed to defer or avoid tax (deferral or postponement being the best that we can achieve) has merit on its own you shouldn't participate.

Tax scams abound. The sad part is that it usually takes years for the investor to be caught and charged with back taxes and penalties. If you hear of a scheme where you can buy something for $10,000 and get a $20,000 tax deduction, something's wrong with this picture. Even if the government accepts your tax return and deduction today, you may be audited in the future and your deduction will be reversed, thus costing you additional tax and probably penalties too. Examples of such schemes include: buying paintings, buying drugs for third world countries, and buying gold coins.

There are many ways in which you can reduce your taxable income legitimately. The scope of this book is too limited to discuss all of the available options but there are some key factors you should be aware of.

Single Mom and children with special needs

As a single mother, you have some tax advantages. You can claim one of your children as equivalent to your spouse. This gives you an additional tax deduction of $10,000 on your tax return. As of this writing, the basic personal tax deduction is $11,038, so an additional $10,000 deduction almost doubles your basic personal deduction.

If your child has a disability you're eligible for an additional $10,000 deduction. So if you're a single parent with a child with a disability, your total base deduction from income will be $31,038. It's rare to find this level of deduction unless you're self-employed or own a business. Please note that the deduction for a child with a disability is not limited to single moms. Any family with a child who has special needs would be eligible for this tax deduction, which would normally be used by the higher income earner.

Taxation on various types of investments

Although this is a complex subject, it's important to understand the basics of how your investments are taxed. There are basically three types of taxation on investments:

- Taxation on interest-bearing investments such as GICs
- Taxation of dividend products, such as dividend stocks or mutual funds that hold dividend stocks
- Taxation of capital gains, such as on the sale of a secondary property or open equity investments

Each of these investment types is taxed differently. Interest-bearing investments are taxed at the highest possible (marginal) tax rate of the holder. Interest is taxable in the year the interest is earned and therefore (unless sheltered within an RRSP or RRIF) must be paid in that year.

Dividend income is taxed at a reduced rate, and is only taxed upon redemption or sale of the investment. Dividend investments also pay out distributions to the investment holding, but remain tax-free until it is sold or deemed as a disposition (eg, upon death).

Capital gains tax may apply to the ownership of various types of property including a cottage (as a second property) or investments that gain in value over time in a non-registered plan. Upon sale or transfer of a holding that triggers a capital gain (ie, increase in value) you'll be subject to tax on only 50% of the capital gain amount. The advantage of capital gains is the reduced tax amount applicable, plus the fact that if there's a capital loss (your investment fell in value) this can be carried forward and used to offset capital gains in the future. When you hold an investment with another person which triggers capital gains, the taxes owed on the capital gains can be divided between the joint owners.

Other ways to save on your taxes

If you're employed by a company and get a regular paycheque with deductions taken off, and a benefits package and possibly a pension, then your tax return is pretty straightforward. There's not a lot of room to take deductions and reduce your taxable income. Ideally, if your company is deducting the correct amount of taxes each year, you should end up with no refund and no taxes owing. Few people consider it lucky to be in this situation, but at least you're not paying too much tax in order to get a refund. When you get a large refund from the government it means you've been letting the government use your money for free. Some people use the refund process as a forced savings, and they can't wait to get that refund to take a trip, buy something new or invest the money in the stock market.

***When it comes to taxation the key word is* reasonable.**

One way to reduce your taxable income is to own a business or be self-employed. There are several legitimate deductions you can make when you're an entrepreneur. For example, you may be able to employ a family member to do administration or computer support, whereby you can deduct the cost of their services. When I say reasonable, I mean that you'd actually employ your partner, invoice them for a reasonable amount, and track what's paid. Your partner would claim this income on their tax return. Conversely, since your three-year-old can't handle customer queries, please don't think of paying them a salary. All things must be reasonable and feasible.

A home-based business has a number of eligible deductions. The Canada Revenue Agency (CRA) expects your income will be greater than your expenses, but it's possible to claim a loss in your first or second year of business. Ongoing losses are not sustainable, however, so don't expect to do this for very long without having to speak to the CRA.

Some major deductions for home-based businesses are related to the space itself. If your home office represents 10% of the overall space in the home, then you can deduct 10% of the operating costs of the home. For example, 10% of your mortgage interest and 10% of utility bills can be deducted from income. The maximum allowable percentage for home-based deductions is (unofficially) 20% in write-offs. Certain expenses such as your phone, internet and cleaning services are 100% deductible.

Your best approach to tracking items for tax purposes is to find out what the CRA wants to see in terms of reporting. For example, if you can deduct the use of your car, you should note, by date, the starting and ending odometer readings. It's not enough to write down the number of kilometers. You must track each trip from start to finish and, as an added bonus; I'd also make note of which client(s) you saw or the purpose of the trip (eg, post office, Staples for supplies). This gives you an ironclad format if you're ever audited by the CRA.

There are similar guidelines for tracking medical expenses. You can never give too much information. Generally medical expenses aren't a huge part of your tax preparation but, if in one year you have four dental implants, then your medical bills could exceed $10,000. This almost guarantees you'll be audited. However, if you've tracked in detail all of your medical expenses on a spreadsheet you'll be fully prepared. Include information such as date, cost of service or prescription, provider and purpose of the medical procedure. Keep all original receipts because if you're audited you'll have to submit a copy of every receipt. You can simplify your accounting by asking your medical provider, eg, dentist, pharmacist, to give you a summary of all services/purchases for the year in one statement.

If you have a child in post-secondary education and they have expenses but no income against which to take tax deductions, the student can transfer the deductions, eg, tuition, to one of their parents. Normally you'd do this with the highest income earner. Alternatively, the expenses can be carried forward for the child to deduct at a future date.

As soon as your children start working, get them to file an income tax return. This will start building their RRSP contribution room. That way, they maximize their RRSP contribution from the beginning and when they start earning a higher income, they get the highest possible deduction for their contribution. The more you make, the more valuable the RRSP tax deduction.

If you borrow money to invest, it's best to keep this loan separate so you can identify and deduct the interest you pay on the loan. Yes, you heard correctly, if you borrow money to invest you can deduct the interest on the investment loan.

Other eligible tax deductions include contributions to political parties and donations to a legitimate charity. In order to deduct charitable donations you need an official receipt with the charity's registration number. Alternatively, if you send a cheque to a charity, note the charity's registration number on your cheque as a form of proof. The receipt or the cancelled cheque with the registration number on it is acceptable. Note that when you purchase an item (baby booties or widgets) from a charity you don't get a tax receipt because it's not considered a tax deductible donation. Donations to your place of worship are also tax deductible and most institutions provide a receipt for any donations that are tracked.

Taxation is a complex area with several ramifications regarding your overall ability to reduce taxes and retain as much of your income as possible. The above information represents only some generic guidelines. I strongly suggest that, unless you have a good foundation in accounting or tax preparation, you should hire a tax accountant to do your taxes at least once or twice so that you're aware of all the possible deductions to reduce income.

Retirement and retirement funding

My sister worked as a Business Systems Analyst for a major technology provider during her final years of working. It was a high-stress job with numerous details to deal with on a daily basis. When she thought about retiring she was terrified that she'd be bored and have nothing to do. Prior to retiring she was very concerned and scared about the whole idea. From a personality standpoint my sister is basically shy and quiet, so getting involved with new groups was automatically a challenge as well.

As she says, "It took me six months before I got involved with outside activities. I really missed the analytical part of the work as opposed to the people part, so I really had to push myself to get involved with the seniors' centre, yoga and the Canadian Federation of University Women (CFUW)."

Within eight months of leaving her full-time job, she was so busy with volunteer work and doing yoga that she barely noticed she'd retired. In fact it's harder for me to book a lunch date with her now than it was when she was working.

Some people see retirement as a death sentence. Others see it as an opportunity to explore new ideas, take up a hobby or spend more time doing their favorite activities. Not only is each person unique, so too are couples when it comes to making retirement plans. Knowing your lifestyle is an important determining factor in estimating your financial needs during retirement.

If traveling is a number one priority, you need to budget accordingly so that withdrawing large sums of money from your retirement savings won't compromise your lifetime financial needs.

Certain information is essential to determining your overall financial needs in retirement. Here are some examples:

- How old are your parents and grandparents?
- If they're deceased, at what age did they die?
- Is there a history of serious illness in the family, eg, heart disease, cancer or Multiple Sclerosis?
- Do you see your doctor annually, eat responsibly and exercise? Do you smoke?
- What are your current monthly overall household costs? How much of this is mortgage? Will your mortgage be paid before you retire?
- Do you plan to work during retirement to supplement your income?
- Will you do volunteer work?
- Do you plan to downsize your home at some point in the future?
- Have you discussed with your family what will happen if you need to go into a retirement home?
- Have you prepared for your demise by having a pre-arranged funeral?
- How much have you saved for retirement? What are your current net worth and the market value of your property?

What do these things have to do with funding your retirement? Your life expectancy, your annual expenses and your current savings all affect your ability to fund your retirement. Understanding family history in terms of longevity and health helps determine how long you're likely to live and whether or not you should have critical illness insurance. Knowing the approximate value of your principal residence and other properties will help determine your potential to liquidate them if needed to fund your retirement.

Because people are living much longer and healthier lives than in the past, there's a greater risk of outliving your money. The calculations to determine your full retirement funding are complicated, requiring special software to be completely accurate. The following is an example of how the rate of return on your investments can drastically change your retirement years.

Here are the assumptions for this example:

- ✓ $500,000 in investable assets for retirement = Total retirement savings
- ✓ Retire at age 65
- ✓ Live to age 90
- ✓ Total income required per month = $4,600 per month
- ✓ Total income from CPP and OAS = $1,600 per month
- ✓ Required withdrawal amount from savings per month = $3,000

If the annual rate of return on the above investment of $500,000 is 5%, then at $3000 per month your money will last 24 years. In other words your money will run out at age 89.

If the annual rate of return on the $500,000 is 6%, your money will last 25 years, until you're age 90.

But if you live to be 92, you'll need an 8% rate of return to make your money last 28 years. As you can see, the rate of return on your investments is a critical aspect of the equation.

This simplified version of calculating funding for retirement doesn't take into account things like cost of living increases, inflation and the use of RRSP funds where withholding taxes apply. The best way to determine your retirement funding needs is to have a comprehensive financial plan done specific to your goals and lifestyle.

Teaching your children about money

If you have children, you probably want to give them the knowledge and skills they need to become self-sufficient. We can help our children develop good lifetime skills by teaching them about finance.

I frequently lecture to high school students about basic finances. I love the interest and enthusiasm these kids have for knowledge about money. Many children today grow up expecting immediate gratification for every want and need. But building a firm financial foundation takes time, patience, energy and dedicated effort. There's no quick fix when it comes to good money sense.

When I was 12 my father said to me, "From now on I'm going to give you your baby bonus cheque (the common name for government-supported child payments at the time) every month, so don't ask me for money ever again."

At that time my baby bonus cheque was eight dollars a month. I had to buy my lunches, clothes and anything else I wanted with that money. So I've been financially independent since I was 12. The world has changed a lot since those days. Although my father's approach was radical, it helped me learn about money very quickly.

I recommend giving today's young teens a sense of responsibility with money. Pay them an allowance or encourage them to work outside the home. Perhaps working for friends or neighbours could be an additional source of income.

Next, teach them what to do with the money they earn. Let's say your daughter makes $12 a week mowing lawns or shoveling snow. Encourage her to put a third of the money aside in a high-yield savings account for some future purchase. One third can then be used immediately for something she wants, like a textbook, and the remaining third could be given to charity or a cause your daughter is passionate about. This approach gives your child a well-rounded appreciation for the use of money, as well as a sense of empowerment about their lives and their ability to affect the world they live in.

SUMMARY

We've come a long way on this journey to knowledge and there've been lots of things to think about. The following is a summary of the key aspects of this book:

Awareness

Just as being self-aware in a physical sense can help to avoid harm, developing money consciousness can help you define your personal relationship with money. Being aware of your finances can help ensure you avoid damaging your credit rating, your budget or your overall life goal achievements. Knowing your net worth, income and expenses will help you make wise decisions about your money.

Avoidance

Once you've established a basic awareness, it's time to ensure that you avoid any situations entailing either physical or financial harm. We avoid a confrontation with someone by thinking on our feet, speaking with the person involved, trying to defuse the situation. We do this to avoid a possibly negative outcome.

In financial matters we avoid getting into a position of financial hardship. By acquiring the correct amount and type of insurance to cover any eventuality, you avoid a financial disaster in advance. The loss of any income in a family setting can have long-term financial effects on your overall life goals. Being properly insured and having a good estate plan will help protect you from these types of financial disasters.

Defence

Knowledge is power, and foreknowledge is the most powerful. Knowledge is learning the definitions, terms and technical details. Wisdom is the application of knowledge to improve your life and that of others. From a financial perspective, defending yourself means doing what's needed to make sure you and your family will be financially secure.

I hope that I've helped in some way to advance your knowledge about financial matters. I've strived to simplify some complex concepts and present them in a way that's easily understood. I wish you light and love on your journey towards financial security.

APPENDIX 1: GLOSSARY OF TERMS

<ins>Canadian:</ins>

The definition of a Canadian is a person born in Canada or a person who moved from somewhere else in the world to become a Canadian. To be Canadian is to accept all others as they are in terms of race, culture, religion and abilities. Being Canadian means you're honest, cheerful and polite as much as possible. We say "sorry" and "excuse me" to a fault. We've been known to wear shorts and a T-shirt outside in the middle of winter. Hockey is our game and we prefer to brawl on the ice rather than take out our anger by warring with our neighbours. As a Canadian you've probably tasted fresh made maple syrup on hot pancakes or even on a ball of snow.

Although we'll fight for our freedom we'd generally rather keep the peace. We have a country so large it can take three days to drive across one province. There are places where your fingers will stick to the door knob in winter, and it's always possible to see a snowstorm in April.

On an international scale many countries accept Canadians with open arms, and although we've been known to embarrass ourselves by overdrinking and acting silly, it's a unique feature of Canada that people from other parts of the world pretend to be Canadians when they travel. This speaks volumes about the respect and attitude that most countries have towards Canada.

We have our flaws, eg, the abysmal treatment of our Indigenous people, our lack of support for efforts against global warming, and the absence of a national policy for the protection of women and children, but Canada is still a great place to live. We need to gather together as a nation and exercise our right to vote to make these things happen.

So, welcome to Canada. I hope that this book can make your transition to your new life in Canada an easier one. Every day there are people trying to move to Canada to improve their lives. Just think - you're already here!! Be proud and happy to be a new Canadian.

APPENDIX 2: PHYSICAL DEFENCE - AWARENESS, AVOIDANCE, DEFENCE

Awareness

- ✓ Know your personal boundaries and comfort level.
- ✓ Learn how to say NO without apology.
- ✓ Be aware of your surroundings at all times.
- ✓ Avoid using cell phones, texting, iPods, etc, when walking or jogging.
- ✓ Never let someone in a bar have access to your drink.
- ✓ Listen to your gut feelings and your instincts.
- ✓ Have a plan for travelling and when out with friends.

Avoidance

- ✓ Do not appear to be an easy target. Walk tall and strong.
- ✓ Always jog, travel or go to bars with friends if possible.
- ✓ Avoid bank terminals and gas stations at night. Favour these services during the day.
- ✓ Avoid situations or circumstances where you may be targeted such as a dark alley at night.
- ✓ Never carry your Social Insurance card (SIN) with you. Memorize your SIN and keep it in a safe place to avoid identity fraud.
- ✓ Meet unknown people in a public place. Especially with online dating.

Defence

- ✓ If it doesn't feel right - GET OUT.
- ✓ Notice areas nearby that are open and public.
- ✓ Remain calm and aware, breathe.
- ✓ Begin by trying to diffuse the situation verbally.
- ✓ Ask the person how you might help. Establish if there's a medical issue. (Diabetic insulin shock appears very similar to someone drunk)
- ✓ Keep your distance and don't corner yourself against a wall.
- ✓ Extend an arm to create personal space.
- ✓ Use a protective stance with two hands up in a non-threatening way (open palm as opposed to fist).
- ✓ Be aware of areas available for escape routes.

✓ Try to draw the attention of others so that they become aware of the situation.

✓ Consider your options and be prepared to move out of the way.

Bottom line: Caution is never cowardice

APPENDIX 3:
EXPENSE WORKSHEET

Please enter the amount that you would spend per month on average for each of these categories. There are blank spaces to add items not listed here.

Shelter	**Monthly Cost**
Rent	
Mortgage Payments	
Property Taxes	
Property Insurance	
Utilities	
Water	
Home Gas/Heating	
Hydro	
Recreational Property	

Renovation/Decor	
Misc. Housing	
Time Share/Condo Fees	
Transportation	
Vehicle Payment	
Gas/Oil	
Repairs	
Car Insurance	
Parking	
Go train/bus passes	
Additional Vehicle expense	
Personal/Family	
Food/Beverage	
Clothing and personal care	
Child Care	
Medical/Dental	
Life Insurance	
Housekeeping	
Weekly spending money	
Misc.	
Liabilities	
Loan Payments	
Credit card payments if carried over monthly	
Other	

Other	
Professional fees	
Travel/Vacation	
Club Membership	
Entertainment	
Charitable Donations	
Gifts	
Phone/Cell/Internet	
Cable/Satellite	
Sports and Leisure	

Once you've totaled your expenses for the month you can compare this to your net income (this is your income after all deductions such as taxes and benefits)

APPENDIX 4: LOVE, MARRIAGE & DIVORCE

Love vs intimacy - What's the difference?

There are many types of love such as the Biblical love *Agape,* the love of a child, and the love between sisters. The love I'm referring to here is the love between two people who evolve to form an ongoing relationship. In the beginning love affects your ability to think rationally. It's the schoolgirl crush in spades! How long it takes to come back to earth depends on your unique relationship. Then comes the comfort phase where life falls into place and you have a routine together. This may be a good thing or it may become boring.

Intimacy in a relationship isn't just about love and physical contact. Having an intimate relationship means you've taken your relationship to a deeper level. There's an inner knowledge and comfort with the person that you are with – a deep knowing trust that this person will never intentionally hurt you. You allow yourself to be vulnerable to this one person who in turn opens to you.

The following is what I call my *Good Marriage Checklist*.

Good marriage	**Not-so-good marriage**
Ongoing communication	Lack of communication
Common principles and values	Differing principles and values
Love and intimacy	Never get to intimacy
Something you need to work at	Just happens
Common interests, many thinks to talk about	Not much in common, no point of discussion
Activities in common – camping, martial arts, playing cards	No activities done as a couple alone (without kids or extended family)
Ability to forgive and move on	Tension mounts from unresolved issues
You pull together when there's disaster, trauma or injury	You deal with disaster individually instead of leaning on each other
You sense each other's moods	You're not in tune with each other
You feel fortified by each other, and know your partner has your back	You feel very alone and not really in a relationship

Joy at togetherness, sadness when apart, but stability either way	Indifferent to each other being around
You change and grow together	As one person changes, you grow apart as a couple

Divorce

Separation, legal or otherwise, can have a devastating effect on your finances. But if it needs to happen, you should prepare yourself rather than blunder into it blindly.

Try to establish your current net worth, your ongoing expenses and what that would look like on your salary alone. Start setting aside a portion of your income to prepare for your exit. Open your own bank accounts and get a separate credit card. If you're a stay-at-home mom, you need to start looking for a job or go back to school to learn a marketable skill.

If you have many young children (making daycare costs prohibitive) consider running a daycare in your home. Establish a home-based business or job share with another mom. There's nothing more empowering than the ability to be "job-proof" and financially independent.

Some suggestions:

- In Ontario, the moment you cease co-habitation, you're considered legally separated. This would not include a court-approved division of assets as yet.
- Protect yourself by knowing your rights.

- Speak with a divorce mediator or lawyer prior to separation.
- Try to settle things as amicably as possible.
- Understand the child custody laws and expectations.
- Know what the Family Responsibility Office (FRO) can do to ensure you receive child support payments, but rely on yourself to meet your own basic financial needs.

People sometimes change and grow apart. Perhaps there are underlying mental issues that neither of you were aware of. Whatever the cause of your divorce, please protect your children from suffering more than is inevitable. Be open with them. Let your children know that this is not their fault. Try to have an amicable division of time with the children for their sake. Keep arguments or disagreements out of their range. This is your divorce, not theirs.

ABOUT THE AUTHOR

Joanne Shaw, BA, CFP

Joanne uses a down-to-earth approach to financial matters. With a Certified Financial Planner (CFP) designation, a degree in Psychology, and over 20 years of martial arts training, Joanne explores our psychology of money and how our personal relationship with money impacts our ability to be financially successful. Money represents power, and being aware of our personal money consciousness enables us to use money in a conscientious way.

Joanne has done numerous speaking engagements and is the author of the Polly Pennywise series of children's books which teach children the basics of finance. Joanne gives volunteer lectures to Grade 10 high school students. She is passionate about educating today's youth and women about the basics of finance. Joanne is currently a financial planner with Canfin Financial Group. You can contact her at jshaw@canfin.com or via her personal website at www.joanneshaw.canfin.com.

17490209R00073

Made in the USA
Middletown, DE
28 November 2018